ROSIE LEWIS

Trapped

The terrifying true story of a young girl's secret world of abuse

HarperElement
An Imprint of HarperCollins*Publishers*
77–85 Fulham Palace Road,
Hammersmith, London W6 8JB

www.harpercollins.co.uk

and *HarperElement* are trademarks of
HarperCollins*Publishers* Ltd

First published by HarperElement 2014

3 5 7 9 10 8 6 4 2

A catalogue record of this book is
available from the British Library

PB ISBN 978-0-00-754178-2
EB ISBN 978-0-00-754179-9

Printed and bound in Great Britain by
Clays Ltd, St Ives plc

MIX
Paper from
responsible sources
FSC C007454

FSC™ is a non-profit international organisation established to promote
the responsible management of the world's forests. Products carrying the
FSC label are independently certified to assure consumers that they come
from forests that are managed to meet the social, economic and
ecological needs of present and future generations,
and other controlled sources.

Find out more about HarperCollins and the environment at
www.harpercollins.co.uk/green

Trapped

Prologue

With small, stumbling fingers Phoebe set her torch on the bedside cabinet, then rolled around her bed until her whole body became swaddled by her sheet, all the way up to her ears. Her cheeks burned with heat but determinedly, she began the awkward process again, this time with her duvet. By the time she had finished breathing was difficult but she felt safe, cocooned from the world outside.

She held herself still for a long time, partly to listen out for danger but mainly because her mummified state wouldn't allow for much movement. The whishing came soon afterwards. At first it was gentle, a bit like the sound she heard when Mummy held a seashell to her ear but then the rustling began, filling her head until she worried that there would be no room left for her brain. The air around her came alive with the patter, drowning everything else out: the loud tick of the big clock in the hall, the muted conversations drifting up through the floorboards, even the whistle of the wind.

Everything in her room remained in the same place; the three-storey doll's house with lifting roof, her white dressing table with the heart-shaped mirror and all the tiny glass perfume bottles lined across the top, and yet in an instant all became unfamiliar. The weak shaft of light from her torch no longer chased shadows into the corners of the room.

She began making funny groans like some of the children at school. The louder she hummed, the more muffled the horrible noise became. And she found that if she spun her eyes around as fast as she could, the pictures in her head got fuzzy too. The hand now pressing on her mouth no longer pinched her cheeks as painfully and the strange words hanging in the air transformed into the fairies that cling to dandelion stems, so light that if she blew hard enough they might float away on the breeze.

As the man dragged her out of her cocoon in one swift movement, chuckling at her attempts to protect herself, she sank deeper into her brain and pictured her father. In her mind he was dressed in his smart suit for work, tall and strong. She longed to call out to him, imagining that he would rush in to pick her up and keep her safe, but sensing that to yell would be dangerous, she bit down hard on her lower lip instead. She told the man that he could chose something from her room, anything he wanted, if only he would go back downstairs and rejoin the party. Her pleading made him laugh again.

Trapped

In the morning it hurt to walk to the bathroom. She moved slowly because her pyjamas were wet and clinging to her legs. As she peeled off her night-clothes she smelt urine and her face grew hot with shame. Mummy would be sure to remove a star from her chart.

The thought brought hot tears to her eyes.

Chapter 1

It was a dreary, overcast day in March 2009 when I first met Phoebe. As I sat in the local authority training centre, I shook my lifeless mobile phone several times, hoping that news of a fostering referral would drift across the airwaves. Between placements I was filled with a restless yearning; an itch I couldn't scratch. How blissfully ignorant I was back then, unaware of the far-reaching impact she would have on our family.

'It would be wise to keep a collection of pebbles in your kitchen drawer,' our lively tutor was drilling us on the latest techniques for safeguarding drug-addicted teenagers. 'That way you'll remember to drop one in if they trust you enough to ask for a bag.'

Ellie was a recent recruit to the local authority team of trainers and a registered nurse by profession. The tall blonde was proving popular with foster carers, her courses particularly well attended by other halves – I had never seen as many men on a training day before. It seemed word of her sultry tones, shiny lip gloss and stiletto heels had worked its way quickly around the fostering network of the north of England.

A flurry of blank looks travelled around the semi-circle of foster carers in front of her.

'We lost one of our teenagers earlier this year,' Ellie went on to explain. 'She passed out with a bag of solvent still fixed to her ears. With a heavy object inside, the plastic would have been far more likely to fall from her face as she collapsed. A little forethought from her carer might just have saved her life.'

'I take it we're expected to provide 'em with a WH Smith voucher as well,' the black foster carer sitting opposite me offered in a Brummie accent, daring a touch of sarcasm, 'to save 'em forkin' out for t'own glue.'

Sniggers swept around the room.

Ellie held out one manicured hand, tucking a stray tendril of shiny blonde hair behind her ear with the other. 'I take it that some of you feel uncomfortable with what I've just said?'

Glancing around, I noticed several of the women nodding their heads. Most of the men sat with their legs sprawled wide, one or two with dreamy expressions on their faces.

'Surely it's our job to discourage risky behaviour?' I ventured. Social workers were keen to encourage foster carers to show Looked After Children the same quality of care as their own families. I was certain that I wouldn't provide bags with rocks inside for my own children, Emily and Jamie, freeing them to get high in the knowledge that Health & Safety procedures had been adhered to by their attentive mother.

Ellie smiled, shaking her head. 'I know it's not easy to stomach but it's our responsibility to safeguard these children. They're damaged – most of them *need* something just to get through the day. Showing disapproval will simply drive their behaviour underground. Having to hide their addiction,' she tilted her dainty hand in mid-air, rocking it slightly from side to side, 'might just be enough to tip them over the edge.'

After a buffet lunch courtesy of the local authority, Ellie moved on to drug classifications and how to recognise paraphernalia among seemingly innocent everyday objects such as empty fizzy drink cans. It was fascinating but her comment about damaged children needing a prop to survive kept playing over in my mind. I felt a longing to soothe the turmoil a child must feel to treat their body with such disregard. The uncomfortable feeling reminded me of why I had decided to register as a foster carer. Like many of my fellow carers, I was drawn to it.

For the rest of the afternoon the class was held rapt, not only by Ellie's dynamic teaching style but also the shocking nature of the facts she was imparting. Between the 20 or so carers present we had chalked up a collective experience of over 200 years of fostering, yet most of us were unaware that the latest trend for self-harmers was to insert diazepam capsules into the cuts in their skin for rapid absorption, or that wheelie bins often went missing because they offered an ideal confined space for solvent abuse.

Most of the training days I had attended in the past fortnight held my attention as efficiently as a pile of wet nappies and so it was refreshing to be presented with such thought-provoking information. It was only towards the end of the day that my concentration began to waver and I idly poked my mobile phone again, willing it to spring into action. My last placement had ended three weeks earlier – a sibling group of two who stayed with me for almost three years. The wounds of separation after they moved on to adoption were still raw, an unfortunate occupational hazard. I was eager to jump back into the saddle of caring again, knowing it was the best way to recover from my loss and so, after taking a break of two weeks, I agreed for my name to reappear on the vacancy register. Recovery time between placements is recommended to restore energy levels; fostering can be a physical and emotional drain. Carers often make use of the time by catching up on training; we are obliged to attend at least six training sessions each year, a tricky task with young ones in placement.

I kept busy during my first week off, getting the house straight, tidying up the garden and attending a round of courses – anything to distract my mind from worrying about how the siblings were coping in their new home. It was such an upheaval for them, leaving all that was familiar behind. When children move on to adoption, it is recommended that their foster carer takes on the role of 'auntie', so remaining part of their lives but in a more distant way. I couldn't help worrying that they might feel abandoned by me and our reunion wasn't to take place for another three weeks, to allow time for their bond with me to weaken. The idea that I would see them again, hopefully happy and settled with their 'forever' parents, gave me something positive to hold on to in the meantime.

For the past week I had been on the out-of-hours list, making myself available to the local authority at any time, day or night, to take on an emergency. So far all had been quiet but I kept my phone close by at all times, just in case.

The timing of the call about Phoebe, when it came, couldn't have been more perfect. I had just completed my course evaluation sheet, giving Ellie top marks in all ten categories, and was wandering out of the training centre into the misty gloom when my mobile phone coughed itself awake.

'Hi, Desmond.' My heart was already beginning to race in anticipation as I climbed into my car with the handset clamped to my ear, wondering whether my supervising social worker had news of an emergency or was simply calling for a chat. We had built up a close friendship since I was first assigned to him when I registered with Bright Heights Fostering Agency seven years earlier and he often popped in to check how our family was, even though he was only strictly obliged to visit once every four weeks.

As I listened to his voice, intermittently thick with a Scottish accent despite having left the Highlands as a teenager, I found myself holding my breath and hoping for a newborn, recklessly forgetting my vow never to take on another baby after my most recent, difficult separation. Reaching to grab a notebook and pen from the dashboard, I jotted down notes as Desmond spoke.

'She's been taken straight from school into police protection. They should be with you in the next half an hour or so. Will you be home by then?'

Slipping the key into the ignition, I switched the Nokia to loudspeaker mode then dropped it into my lap. 'Yes, should be. I'll just have enough time to let Emily and Jamie know what's going on.'

My own children were keen to welcome new little ones into our home but I preferred to seek their approval before someone new arrived on the doorstep, to make sure they felt consulted.

'I won't be able to make it, I'm afraid – sorry, Rosie, I'm up to my neck in it over here. I'll come and see you some time in the next few days, though.'

Saying goodbye to Des, I stopped at the next set of traffic lights, holding my notebook up at eye level. The page was still blank but for my scribbled notes: girl, age eight; warm and friendly. Without noticing the lights as they turned to amber, I sat staring at the words on the page. Overstretched social workers were sometimes so keen to place a child that they stretched the facts, I mused, moulding them into a mishmash of half-truths and downright fabrications. Experience had taught me to treat the initial information they provided on a child with as much caution as estate agents' patter. Just as a house located at the side of a busy motorway could be listed as 'close to all transport links', social workers might describe a difficult, confrontational teenager with a penchant for injecting heroin as 'lively and inquisitive'.

A hoot from the driver behind caused me to start. Lifting my hand in apology, I nudged the accelerator and caught up with the rusting white van ahead, catching sight of myself in the rear-view mirror. Often I felt that my blonde, naturally curly hair offered a cheery distraction from the lines that were beginning to appear under my eyes, giving people the impression that I was bubbly even when I felt nothing of the sort. Today, though, the damp air had taken its toll, making it look like a pile of dried hay and dragging the rest of my face down with it. Grimacing, I tucked the frizz behind my ears, hoping to fit in a hair wash before Phoebe's arrival.

Driving under an arched railway bridge and along a tree-lined, residential side road I noticed a few drops of rain appearing on the windscreen. A grimly portentous grey sky stretched into the distance and a bubble of apprehension rose in my stomach as I flicked the wipers on, knotting itself stubbornly in my throat. 'Warm and friendly' were hardly forbidding adjectives, so what was I reading between the lines?

Chapter 2

My 11-year-old son Jamie arrived home a few minutes after me. On hearing the news he dashed into the kitchen, armed himself with some biscuits then took up a position leaning over the back of the sofa, staring out of the living-room window. With Jamie as self-appointed lookout I fussed around the spare room, trying to make it look as welcoming as possible for the new arrival. With the police involved, and Phoebe being taken without the consent of her parents, it was likely she would arrive in a highly distressed state.

Planned placements were much easier to prepare for than emergencies, with time to find out the child's interests. With so little warning, it was difficult to tailor the bedroom to appeal especially to Phoebe. The airing cupboard was full of duvet covers and curtains I had collected over the years, with everything from Fireman Sam to Peppa Pig, but what would a warm and friendly eight-year-old like? I wondered, finally settling on a cover featuring Disney's Beauty and the Beast.

Tense with anticipation, I jumped at the sound of a key in the door.

'Mum?'

It was my 14-year-old daughter Emily, just home from school.

'Guess what, Em?' I called out.

She darted up the stairs and arrived on the landing, rain-soaked blonde hair flattened against her flushed cheeks, rucksack still half-slung over her shoulder.

'We got a call?'

I nodded, smiling. It was lovely to see her so excited. 'She's eight years old and friendly, that's about all I know at the moment.'

'Great!' Throwing a soggy arm around my neck, she dropped her rucksack on the carpet, draped her damp blazer over the bannister and dashed past me into the spare room.

Flitting in and out of the space, she arranged soft toys on every available surface. Twisting a set of lights around the struts at the foot of the bed, she announced a sudden brainwave. 'I still have my old stick-arounds, pink butterflies and stuff. We could decorate the walls to make it look more girlie in here.'

'Lovely idea,' I said as she rushed past me en route to her own bedroom. I was grateful that she and Jamie remained as committed to fostering as I was. In any fostering family, birth children sometimes get overlooked. Foster children can demand a high level of attention but Emily and Jamie never seemed to resent having to share my time – they just seemed to want to make life better for whoever stayed with us, particularly the most troubled youngsters. I regularly reminded them that by being friendly and welcoming, they helped to do just that.

'Did they say how long she'd be staying?' Emily asked, breathlessly separating sticky butterflies from the dusty packet she had retrieved from her room.

I pictured my scribbled notes and shook my head. Actually I knew very little about Phoebe and certainly had no idea how long the placement would last, but that was often the way. When children arrive as an emergency, the on-call foster carer is obliged to keep them for 72 hours, but as I had a vacancy it made sense for Phoebe to stay with us for as long as necessary.

As I was a short-term foster carer, the placement could last anything from one night to four or five years. The aim of short-term or 'task-based' fostering is to support the child through the uncertain stage when their birth family is being assessed by the local authority; if a Care Order is secured through the courts, the child needs to be primed for permanency with long-term carers.

With the room ready, Emily followed me downstairs and into the living room. I sank into the sofa and she flopped beside me. 'I wish they'd hurry up,' she said, laying her head on my shoulder.

My whirlwind son, Jamie, was far less effusive in his excitement. 'Why couldn't it have been a boy?' he asked from his position on the two-seater sofa, though he still tapped out a rhythm on the window sill with restless fingers, eager to catch a first sight of his new housemate. 'Girls are boring.'

I smiled to myself. While Emily was a sensitive soul, contemplative and always receptive to the feelings of others, my son says what he sees. 'You know where you are with Jamie,' was a comment made by several of his teachers. I presume it was a compliment.

'Right, so we all remember the safe caring rules, don't we?'

Jamie clapped a hand to his forehead. 'Oh, heck, here we go,' he groaned. 'We're not stupid, Mum!'

'It's important that we protect ourselves, Jamie, as well as Phoebe.' I knew that they both tired of being reminded to stay out of all bedrooms except their own and to avoid physical 'horseplay' with the foster children but it was so easy to forget, especially once the children have settled and everyone adjusts to the new dynamics of having an extra person around.

An exhilarated excitement buzzed through my veins, as it did at the beginning of every placement. Everything to come would be new and mysterious, offering our family a whole new set of challenges. Before the year was out we would encounter an extreme range of disturbing behaviours and Phoebe would be one of the most extraordinary, heartbreaking placements we had ever taken on.

But in the companionable peace of our cosy living room, I had no sense of the enormity of what we were about to face.

Chapter 3

It was Jamie who first spotted something was amiss.

He was standing excitedly at the window to watch for her arrival, and I could tell by the quiver in his voice that the young girl walking up the path wasn't at all what he was expecting.

'Mum, she's … er, Phoebe's here.'

With the sound of my own heartbeat rushing in my ears I reached the door as the bell rang, giving me just enough time to smooth down my unruly, unwashed hair. 'Hello, Phoebe,' I said, the friendly smile on my face stiffening as I caught sight of the 120 centimetres of disgruntlement standing on the doorstep. One glance told me that the description 'warm and friendly' might have been a tad overgenerous.

'*Hello, Phoebe*,' she mimicked with a sneer before barging past me into the hall.

'Goodness, well, come in,' I said, with false brightness. All of the children I have looked after have exhibited some level of 'challenging' behaviour but on first arriving in a new placement, most were withdrawn; only once they felt safe enough to test the boundaries did the difficult behaviour begin to emerge, signalling the end of the honeymoon period.

It was the first sign that Phoebe would turn everything I thought I knew about childcare completely on its head.

Lenke, Phoebe's social worker, hovered on the path. She was a rotund, bosomy woman, and I groaned inwardly as I stepped aside and welcomed her in. The previous year the Hungarian social worker had been responsible for a child I had accepted for a fortnight's respite and though I'd got on fine with her, I formed the strong impression that her heart really wasn't in the job. Besides a laissez-faire attitude, she didn't seem to have a clue what she was doing.

Whatever I had asked for, whether it was GP details or a contact schedule, a blank expression would cross her face, followed by a futile search through the dog-eared contents of her overlarge leather bag. A sketchy command of the English language on top of her air of disinterest was one complication too many and in short, communication had been a trifle frustrating.

A loud chanting from the living room quickened my step along the hall.

'Jamie, Jamie, Jamie! Wet willy, wet willy!'

'Lovely it is to see you again, Rosie,' Lenke said breezily to my back, as though the walls of the hallway were not vibrating with the sound of piercing screeches coming from the living room.

The first thing I noticed when I stood in the doorway was the horrified expression on my son's face. He was arching over the back of the sofa, fending Phoebe off with his arms as she fought to stick her wet finger in his ear.

'Stop that please, Phoebe,' I said, my voice sharp. Clearly there was to be no honeymoon period in this placement and the sooner she learnt who was in charge, the better.

'*Stop that please, Phoebe*,' she mimicked again. Although she was using a high-pitched, scornful tone, I could tell immediately that she was well-spoken, each word precisely clipped. Thankfully my own tone had an effect. Although she fixed me with a brazen look she stopped what she was doing and began staring at me with a nasty, twisted smile on her face.

'I'm going to my room,' Jamie wheezed. He passed me with his head bent over so I couldn't see his expression but the slope of his shoulders told me how he was feeling. Despite his protestations about wanting a boy, I knew he had been looking forward to meeting Phoebe.

'OK, Jamie, that's fine,' I said, my voice tight as a sudden guilt clawed at my throat. What had I taken on here?

'I'm going too.' Phoebe flipped over the sofa and charged across the room but I stepped backwards to fill the doorway by stretching out my arms.

'No.' I summoned my most commanding tone. 'We don't go into each other's rooms. Now go and sit down. I'll show you around the house later, if you sit nicely while I talk to Lenke.'

'*Sit nicely while I talk to Lenke*,' she repeated, spinning around and returning to the sofa. Lenke walked past and I gestured for her to take a seat. The social worker headed for the opposite end of the sofa, hardly looking at Phoebe, who sat with her legs sprawled, glaring at me. Her hair was brown and frizzy-looking. The style was boyish, cut short to make the wiry texture more manageable, I imagined. Her eyes were appealing, light brown in colour, but seemed to swivel, giving her a slightly deranged look, and she was scarily thin, so much so that the skin across her cheekbones had a translucent quality.

'How about we find some colouring for you to do, Phoebe?' I said, crossing the room. 'Emily, would you mind fetching the pens and some paper? Phoebe can sit at the table while Lenke and I chat through some of the boring details.'

Emily was watching Phoebe, intrigued. 'Sure,' she answered, giving me a sidelong glance. 'Come on, Phoebe.'

'*Come on, Phoebe*,' she chorused. Emily giggled in response and out of nowhere I remembered reading *A Series of Unfortunate Events* to her when she was younger. One of the characters in the book, the headmaster, mocked everything the Baudelaire children said. His outlandishly rude character had captured Emily's imagination at the time and she found it hilarious. I wondered if she was thinking the same as me.

'Would you like tea, coffee?'

'No, it is fine.' Lenke waved her hand and pulled her substantial coat a little tighter around herself. She looked distinctly uncomfortable. The social worker wants this over with, I realised, as I sat next to her on the sofa.

'So,' I said in hushed tones once Phoebe was settled at the dining table. Our house is open-plan so even though I could still see her, she was out of earshot. 'What's the story with Phoebe?'

'Oh,' Lenke waved her hand dismissively. 'Phoebe, she has a touch of, er, what you say?'

I shook my head.

'Er,' she hesitated then reached into her bag, pulling out her diary and flicking through it as if the word she was looking for would miraculously leap from the page. 'I do not have the, what is it, the papers yet. It was all such an emergency. But it is, er, I think you say autism?'

'Autism?' I said, louder than intended. Phoebe inclined her head, staring at me with a strange grin on her face and then, without warning, she threw her head back and began barking. 'That wasn't mentioned by the agency,' I said over the din. Of course, autism would explain her erratic behaviour. The mimicking, screeching and barking made much more sense now.

'Well, it's how you say, erm, mildly, not much autistic.'

'Really?' In the background I could see Phoebe flapping her arms in front of herself like a demented penguin. That could never be described as mild, I thought drily, not in any language. Emily was watching the antics of the new arrival, her eyes wide with fascination.

'Why was she taken into police protection?'

Lenke watched my lips avidly. 'Excuse me?'

'I said …' I raised my voice again to compete with the animal noises coming from across the room. Phoebe fixed me with another icy stare. 'Why has she been removed?'

'Er, she is, erm, telling one of her teachers today that her mum hurt her arm. She twist it behind her back, so she say.'

'Is she known to social services already?'

'Sorry? I don't know this …'

'Is she subject to a Child Protection Order?'

'Oh no, no,' Lenke shook her head. 'This family is fine, no problems. Her father is very successful financier. Respectable. I think that this is possibly false alarm. It may be, erm, possibly part of the illness. We interview the parents this afternoon. They are mortified, really. Nice people, yes. She should be able to go home as …'

A scream from across the room stopped Lenke in mid-sentence. The noise was somewhere between a balloon squeak and a smoke alarm. 'Please, Phoebe,' I said evenly but kept my tone stern, 'don't scream, sweetie. It's upsetting.'

'*Don't scream, it's upsetting*,' she repeated contemptuously, but picked up another pen and returned to her colouring.

Lenke smiled serenely, the picture of innocence. 'I think it be good for her parents to have a break. When she back home we will look into the, how you say,' she fluttered her hand through the air, as if trying to catch the right word, 'you know, a rest?'

'Respite?' I offered.

Lenke nodded emphatically. In the background Phoebe began flapping again, this time accompanied by a loud 'whoop-whoop' noise. I could certainly understand how her parents may have reached the end of their tether, dealing with such severe problems on a daily basis. We're going to have our work cut out here, even just to get through a few days, I thought rather guiltily. Still, Phoebe was just a little girl and we would have to make the best of it. I had dealt with difficult situations before, I reassured myself. There had been times in the past when I had been daunted by difficult behaviour but with patience and support from my family we had managed to overcome whatever problems we encountered.

Within half an hour I had signed several copies of the Placement Planning Agreement. Most of the form was blank since so little was known about Phoebe but the basic facts were there, along with her parents' details. Their address caught my attention – Rosewood Drive, a rather prestigious road several miles from us, with manicured lawns and substantial houses. So, the family must be fairly well-to-do, I thought to myself, which tied in with her well-spoken accent. Most of the children I had cared for in the past were from impoverished backgrounds.

Every family has its problems, I mused. 'Is she on any medication to control her …?' But Lenke zipped up her bag, then stood, tying her belt around her coat. I guess that's a no then, I thought. She began drifting from the room, her relief palpable.

'Well, that is all I know for now. I'll leave you to it, Rosie. Bye bye, Phoebe.'

Phoebe barked in response.

'Good luck, Rosie,' Lenke called out over her shoulder as I stood on the doorstep, waving her off. 'Ah, I forgot to mention one more thing: the school says that Phoebe has the condition called pica so you need to be careful about leaving her unsupervised.' I stared at her agog but she scuttled down the path without a backward glance. She may as well have shouted, 'See you, wouldn't want to be you!' Not for the first time since I received the initial call about Phoebe, I was filled with a growing trepidation.

I remembered from our initial training that children with pica were inclined to eat inedible objects. I had no personal experience of the condition but guessed it meant that Phoebe would have to be treated like a toddler: any object could be a potential choking hazard. I was beginning to understand how difficult it must have been for her parents to cope with her.

It was as I closed the door that a strange groaning noise from the dining room drew me back. Emily called out, 'Mum, I think maybe you should come here …'

Rushing back into the room I noticed the look of concern on Emily's face as she watched Phoebe standing on the table with her legs spread wide, loudly remonstrating with thin air. Her arms flailed wildly as she spewed words out in no meaningful order – 'You get that off, pens so useless, rip it out, bitch!'

'Are you alright, Phoebe?' Emily asked, moving forwards before I could form the words to stop her.

Phoebe screamed, kicking Emily's outstretched arm, hard.

Chapter 4

'*We don't kick in this house*,' Phoebe mimicked in response to my admonishment, her lip curled into an ugly sneer. She stared at me with defiance, her feet still firmly planted on the dining room table.

Following her brother's recent footsteps, Emily had disappeared upstairs, shocked by the violence of Phoebe's outburst. I forced myself to take a few deep breaths, my mind racing to come up with a strategy to deal with her behaviour. Making a mental note to research autism as soon as I had the time, I summoned a commanding tone. 'Get down from the table, please, Phoebe. I'd like to show you around.'

As I spoke I ran through my discipline options if she refused to move. My mind drew a blank but fortunately she climbed down, giving me a flinty, hard stare. 'Good girl,' I said, forcing a bright tone. 'Now, let's show you where you'll be sleeping.'

A shadow crossed her features, giving me a brief glimpse of a little girl lost, but a moment later it had gone, replaced by the same disturbing glare. 'Woof, grrrr, woof.' Phoebe followed, close at my heels. I sensed it would be futile to ask her to be quiet so I raised my voice above hers and launched into my standard welcoming speech, hoping she might be interested enough to stop.

'This is Emily's room,' I said as we passed my daughter's bedroom. I pictured Emily nursing her sore arm on the other side of the closed door and a wisp of anger rose to my throat. Seeing your own children physically hurt is a bitter pill to swallow, especially when they put up with so much anyway. Phoebe's just a young girl with a complex medical disorder, I reminded myself, she probably doesn't even register what she's done.

'We don't go into each other's rooms, ever. If I'm in my bedroom and you need me, you must knock on the door and wait, OK?'

Some of my fellow foster carers had been through the anguish of having allegations made against them and I wanted to protect my own family from a similar fate as vigorously as I possibly could. Of course, following the rules by keeping the children out of each other's bedrooms could never provide full immunity from malicious allegations but by following the guidelines and keeping meticulous daily records, I was doing as much as I could to protect us all.

'*Knock on the door and wait, OK*?'

'And this is Jamie's,' I said.

'This is Jamie's.'

I stared at her, wondering whether she even understood me, although something in her eyes told me that she was taking in every word I said. I remembered reading somewhere that some autistic children could be very bright. It would be helpful to hear what her teachers had to say about her but as the Easter holidays were about to start that wouldn't be possible. Going by what Lenke had said, Phoebe would be back with her family before the start of the summer term so I knew I might not get the chance at all.

Phoebe charged clumsily along the hallway but when we reached her room she hovered in the doorway, suddenly reserved.

'It's alright,' I told her. 'You can go in. Have a look around – this is where you'll be sleeping. It's a safe place. No one will come into your room except me, and only when you want me to. If you prefer me to wait at the door then I will.'

She turned slowly towards me, suddenly bereft. 'I want to go home,' she said, her bottom lip quivering.

'I know, sweetie,' I said, all irritation gone. For the first time since she'd arrived she looked like an ordinary, fragile girl. No eye swivelling, flapping of arms or yelping. I felt a flash of relief knowing there were times when she could be still, if only for a moment. Reaching out, I touched the back of her head, hoping the gesture would communicate my solidarity. She flinched, darting out of the way.

What did you do that for? I chastised myself. Knowing nothing of her history, I should have known better than to offer her physical comfort. Perhaps her parents were a bit heavy-handed with her, I thought, if the way she recoiled from me was anything to go by.

Lowering myself to my knees at the threshold of her room, I beckoned her over. She shook her head, backing away and barking loudly like a resentful Rottweiler guarding its territory. When she reached the wall she crouched, lowering herself to her haunches. Her barks subsided to little yaps.

'Phoebe, can I come in and give you a hug?'

A look of puzzlement crossed her face and my heart went out to her. She seemed so lost. Tempted to sit beside her and take her onto my lap, I hesitated, waiting for her agreement. She stayed silent so I rocked back onto my outstretched feet instead; it would be wrong to assume she wanted comfort from someone she barely knew.

'Phoebe, you're safe here, honey. Do you understand?'

The tiniest nod told me that she'd heard so I reached around the corner and grabbed a notepad from the bookshelf beside her bed. 'Good. Now, this notepad is especially for you. On one page I'd like you to write down all the foods you really don't like and then I'll make sure I don't give them to you. On the other side you can make a list of your favourites. Is that OK?'

She shook her head and began barking again.

'Does that mean no?' I knew that food was one of the issues that children found most frightening when coming into care. The upheaval of leaving home, being separated from their parents and having to adjust to a whole new environment full of strangers was daunting enough. To then be confronted with strange, unfamiliar food seemed to be the tipping point for many children, often making their first mealtimes a traumatic experience, with lots of tears.

In the past I had found the tension at the dinner table could be avoided by finding out beforehand what the children liked to eat. Phoebe continued to shake her head and I wondered about the extent of her learning disabilities. Developmental delays weren't unusual in children who were brought into care, although Phoebe, coming from a middle-class background, wasn't a typical example of a Looked After Child. I knew the latest neuroscience research suggested that high levels of stress in infants could have a damaging impact on the brain, affecting future learning. Perhaps she was unable to write?

'I only eat porridge.'

'That's fine,' I said, in a reassuring tone. 'Porridge makes a great breakfast – we often have porridge too. But what else do you like to eat? Pizza? Roast, maybe?'

Phoebe began to retch, her throat making sickening noises as she heaved. Her eyes bulged and she leaned over, projecting the contents of her stomach over the carpet. She flapped her arms as if in a spasm, spattering the vomit that clung to her fingers all around the room.

I couldn't believe how quickly the vomiting came on. As I leapt towards her she howled, her eyes swivelling back to reveal the whites. I grabbed hold of her hands to stop her from dancing in the mess but she fought away.

'No, please, leave me, no!'

'It's alright, sweetie. Come to the bathroom and I'll clean you up.'

My hands were sticky with vomit and my own stomach lurched as a foul smell rose to my nostrils. Guiding her into the bathroom, I held my breath and began filling the bath. Squeezing a generous amount of bath gel into the water, I swirled it around, knowing she would probably feel more comfortable in the water if it was full of bubbles.

'Right, get those clothes off, sweetie.'

Phoebe began to pant, backing herself into the corner of the room. She looked terrified.

'Would you prefer to clean yourself up?' I tried to keep my voice even, soothing. I wasn't surprised that she might feel too self-conscious to undress in front of a stranger, but why panic-stricken? She looked up at me with bulging eyes and gave an almost imperceptible nod.

'OK, I'll go and clean up your room. There's soap and shampoo on the side. Call me if you need me, won't you?'

I hesitated for a moment but she didn't move so I walked out, leaving the door slightly ajar.

After conducting a hurried clean-up in her room I knocked on the bathroom door.

'All OK in there, honey?'

There was no answer. I guessed that she had her ears under the water, rinsing off shampoo.

'Phoebe?' Ducking my head around the door, I gasped in shock. 'Phoebe, *no*!'

Lunging towards the bath, I snatched the open bottle of bubble bath from her hands. Blood sprung from her lip and

I realised that I must have caught her gum on the rim of the container as I yanked it away. Clamping her fingers over her mouth, she stared at me in horror.

'I'm sorry, I didn't mean to hurt you, Phoebe, but you mustn't drink that. It'll make you ill.'

She lowered her hand, staring at the string of bloody saliva entwined around her fingers. I expected her to cry but she continued to gape as droplets of blood spilt from her mouth into the bath water. Her whole body was trembling.

'Did you hear me, Phoebe?' I said, the metallic taste of panic filling my voice with urgency. She didn't answer but a strange gurgling sound came from her throat. I began to tremble myself, worried that the thick liquid might congeal in her airways and choke her.

'Don't move. I'll be right back.'

I dashed out of the bathroom and downstairs, grabbing a carton of milk from the fridge. If there were harsh chemicals in the potion, I guessed that milk might be the gentlest way to dilute the effects. As I darted back up the stairs my mind came up with a dozen catastrophic scenarios. What if she'd decided to start on the shampoo while I was gone? What if she lay convulsing on the other side of the door? Charging back into the bathroom, I was relieved to find Phoebe wedged between the toilet bowl and the bath. She was still naked and trembling with cold, her thin legs hugged protectively to her chest. Draping a small hand towel around her shoulders wasn't easy in the confined space but I did the best I could.

'Here, drink this,' I said in a shaky voice. 'It'll make your throat and tummy feel better after drinking that yucky stuff.'

She shook her head, recoiling from me. I forced a soothing tone.

'Come on, sweetie, have some milk and then we'll go and explore the garden.'

She looked at me, unmoving. At the best of times it can be frustrating when a child flatly refuses to do as they are told. When their safety is at risk it can be exasperating. My usual coercion strategy is to make sure I have a few treats planned so that I can use them as leverage but at that moment there wasn't any time for mind games.

I was tempted to grab her by the shoulders and yell, 'DRINK IT!' but instead I took a few calming breaths and reached for the empty bottle, scanning the label for advice. *Avoid contact with eyes. If product enters eyes, rinse immediately with warm, clean water* was all it said, but nothing about what to do if a vulnerable child whose care had been entrusted to you takes it into her head to down the half-full bottle in one.

'Phoebe, please,' I said, not too proud to use a begging tone. 'Drink some milk and then we'll get you dry.'

'*Drink some milk and then we'll get you dry*,' she gurgled back, her pupils wide and staring.

Irritation cleared my head and I held up a large bath towel.

'Come on then, up you get.'

Her bony hand darted out and she grabbed the towel, wrapping it around herself in a half-crouched position. The ends of the towel draped into the bath and over the toilet seat. When she finally stood up the floor got a soaking but at that moment a slip hazard was the least of my problems. Not wanting to let her out of my sight, I darted into my bedroom to grab the cordless telephone and guided her back into her own room.

'You get dried and dressed while I make a phone call. Don't worry, I won't look.'

'*Don't worry, I won't look.*' Her voice rippled as though speaking underwater. Clasping the towel tightly around herself she went to her suitcase and rifled through the clothes. It struck me as peculiar that she showed no concern for her own welfare: when my own children were unwell, if they ever caught on that I was worried about them, they would ask endless questions, seeking reassurance. But it seemed as if Phoebe didn't remotely care that she might be in danger. I wondered whether she lacked the mental capacity to understand the consequences of her actions.

A quick call to our local surgery reassured me that there was no need to dash to the hospital for an emergency stomach pumping. According to the doctor, children's bubble bath was non-toxic and unlikely to cause any long-term damage but he did suggest that Phoebe drink plenty of milk or water and told me to keep an eye out for any further symptoms.

Before she went to bed that night I conducted a sweep of the room, removing anything I thought she might be tempted to nibble on and unwinding the decorative lights that Emily had twisted around the foot of the bed. I was still fretting about what might be going on in her stomach. She hadn't eaten a morsel since arriving hours earlier, nothing edible at least. No wonder she was so thin, I thought. I had managed to persuade her to drink half a cup of milk, though only through a straw. She gagged whenever I tried to tempt her into eating anything else, heaving at the mere mention of food.

Consuming bubble bath was one thing but I worried that if she was really hungry she might decide to snack on something solid during the night. If an object slipped down her throat, how on earth would I know about it before the morning? The thought paralysed me and as I stood at the door and watched her climb into bed that night I almost sighed with relief at the temporary reprieve.

'Goodnight, sweetie. Now, you mustn't put anything in your mouth, OK? I'm just down the hall if you need me.'

As I went downstairs I felt as if I was lowering myself into a narrow box, the sides closing in around me and the lid nailed down by unseen hands. It may sound strange but at the beginning of every placement I've taken on, there has been a short period when I've felt trapped by my decision to foster. I guess it's a natural reaction – it feels surreal to suddenly be responsible for another human being, especially when there is absolutely no connection between you.

Thankfully, I have managed to build a rapport with each of the children I've cared for in a short space of time, usually within a few days. As each relationship strengthened, I found that the claustrophobia ebbed away. The trouble was, with Phoebe, I just couldn't see it happening. Down in the living room, I visualised the virtual calendar I had in my head; she would be gone before the end of the Easter holidays – one day down, 13 to go.

Chapter 5

The next morning I woke at just after 6am, feeling a bit more positive. Phoebe had slept right through the night, something I hadn't expected at all. Most children struggled to settle for the first few nights in a strange bed and so I had been prepared for some degree of sleep deprivation.

Relishing the silence, I washed and dressed then pottered downstairs and made myself a coffee. Sitting at the kitchen table, I watched a pair of robins settling on the branch of our apple tree, their wings shining in the bright, early morning sunshine. The scent of winter jasmine floated through the open window, boosting my already lightened mood. As I sipped my warm drink, I dared to think that the placement might not be as difficult as I had first thought. With firm boundaries in place, Phoebe's symptoms might not be so pronounced as they were on her arrival. I wasn't that knowledgeable about autism but I had heard that routine went a long way in helping sufferers to cope with the everyday stresses that other children barely noticed.

And anyway, that was the nature of fostering; no one ever said it would be straightforward. Whatever the reason for their removal from home, fostered children arrive in placement at probably one of the lowest points in their lives. It's not surprising that they may then 'act out' their unhappiness, perhaps by stealing food, money or items of sentimental value, destroying property, refusing to wash, being deliberately provocative, violent or aggressive, or more passively, wetting the bed or self-harming. But having a hand in helping a child to mend was hugely satisfying and certainly worth all the hardships along the way.

That's not to say there is always a happy ending. It took me a while to accept that. Alfie, for instance, whose mother was imprisoned for a short period for his neglect, stayed with me about four years earlier, while a Care Order was secured through the courts. Members of his wider family were assessed and it was decided to award his grandmother special guardianship. I have since heard through the grapevine that Alfie's mother left prison and went straight to live with her own mother in the flat where she cared for Alfie.

Within weeks a new young boyfriend had joined her there and recently grandmother (who hadn't yet celebrated her fortieth birthday) fell for a roofer from Essex and spent long periods of time drinking with him in his bedsit in Hornchurch. I have known social services to spend two years and an inordinate amount of money securing a Care

Order through the courts, only for the children to then return home via obliging friends or relatives. It's not an ideal system.

It is sometimes said that foster carers are 'in it for the money'. I find it difficult to believe that anyone could survive more than six months as a foster carer unless there was a powerful drive to 'heal' hurt children.

For one child, a foster carer's 'wage' is around £200 per week, although this amount varies depending on the local authority. On top of that an allowance of between £60 and £100 is paid (depending on the age of the child), an amount that must be spent solely on the child and meticulously accounted for. Surviving on £800 a month can be a struggle, particularly in a one-parent household. With two children in placement, life is a bit more comfortable but certainly not luxurious.

I've never been driven by money; for me a happy home life and contented children holds far more value and so being able to just about manage was all I needed to be content. Fostering had given me many 'I will never *ever* forget this' moments, some of them for their awfulness, but others that were almost magical.

By 7.30am I was beginning to find the stillness unsettling. In my experience it was unusual for the under-10s to sleep in. Reluctant to disturb the blissful peace but unable to relax without checking on Phoebe, I crept up the stairs and along the hall. The smell hit me before I reached her closed door and I groaned, anticipating the scene before I had even laid my hand on the handle.

It was worse than I'd thought.

Retching as violently as Phoebe had done the evening before, I clamped my hand over my mouth and forced my feet to shuffle into the room, flicking the light switch on with my elbow. Phoebe lay serenely in bed, the duvet pulled up to her neck just as it was when I left her the night before. The room was considerably different, though: the magnolia walls were smeared with streaks of excrement, each lilac butterfly spattered with a generous coating of stomach-churning brown. Even the curtains hadn't escaped Phoebe's attention, with clumps of stinking excrement clinging to the fabric.

I couldn't help myself: 'My God, what have you done?'

'*My God, what have you done*?'

That was it. I charged into the room and yanked the duvet away from her. Phoebe squealed, drawing her soiled hands up to her cheeks and rolling to one side. Curled up in a foetal position, she buried her face in her stained and smelly pillow. My fury ebbed away at the sight of her lying there, so thin and pitiful. Instantly I felt ashamed that I'd broken my promise by entering her room without being invited. Still panting in shock, I stared down at her, frowning. There was something different about her, though, and it wasn't just the streaks of brown across her hands.

'Phoebe, you need to get out of bed so I can clean you up,' I said, my voice wobbling with the strain of keeping my feelings of revulsion under control. She pushed herself up to a sitting position, watching me warily. As she stood up I realised what had changed; she looked bulkier, as if she'd put on half a stone overnight.

'What have you got on under those pyjamas?' I demanded, wondering what other horrors might yet be uncovered.

'*What have you ...?*'

'That's enough,' I shouted, my finger raised and pointing at her. 'I don't want you to copy me, do you hear? Now go to the bathroom, right now!'

Without warning she ducked and ran past me, out of the room. I tried to grab her but she was too quick, darting out of reach.

'Phoebe, come back,' I called, trying to sound firm but unthreatening. Holding my breath, I followed the brown prints her soiled feet had made on the cream carpet. The air smelt vile.

'What's all the noise, Mum?' Jamie's timing couldn't have been more devastating. Bleary-eyed, he sauntered out of his room as Phoebe tore along the hall, holding out his hands in a defensive action as she flapped her arms through the air. His look of horror told me that he realised exactly what she was covered in.

'Sorry, Jamie,' I muttered, charging past him and, with damage limitation at the forefront of my mind, followed Phoebe down the stairs.

'Urgh, she is sooooo disgusting!' Jamie, usually so mild-mannered, wailed angrily from upstairs. 'Come and have a look at her room, Mum.'

Ignoring him, I followed Phoebe into the living room, desperate to catch her in case she nursed an intention of sprawling herself out on one of the sofas in all her self-decorated glory. There was no sign of her there so I quickly scanned the dining area, half-aware of Jamie's bewildered shouts of disbelief floating down from upstairs. 'Mum, really, you've got to come and see this. You won't believe what she's done in here.'

'Eww-urgh!' Another horrified shriek announced Emily's emergence from her room. 'Mum, what's happened to my butterflies?'

Phoebe was crouched in the corner of the kitchen, her face full of fear. She held her dirty hands protectively in front of her.

Ten minutes later Phoebe sat in the bath with the door open while I gathered together every cleaning product in the house to spray, squirt and obliterate the smell permeating each room. Jamie hunkered down in his room with Emily. I was pleased that they had chosen to recover from their shock together. The pair had always shared a good relationship and it seemed that bad experiences brought them even closer. I could hear their urgent chatter drifting beneath the closed door, low tones interspersed with manic giggles.

As I scrubbed Phoebe's soiled room, I was gripped by regular heaving fits: it wasn't only the acrid smell – every time I set about cleaning a new area, the mess spread. What it really needed was a power hose.

Every few minutes I stopped what I was doing and peered around the bathroom door to make sure Phoebe wasn't feasting on anything she shouldn't. After the 'Bubble

Gate' affair I had cleared the bathroom of anything that wasn't nailed down but there was a chance I might have overlooked something. For all I knew, even the bath plug might be adequate fodder in her eyes.

The hollow gaps above her clavicles were so deep with undernourishment that the bath water pooled there as she sat up. Resolving to try and tempt her into eating with double chocolate pancakes for breakfast, I leaned into the bathroom and, with reluctant, pincered fingers, picked up her discarded pyjamas from the floor. Her soiled knickers were knotted up with the legs so I tried to separate the items, realising there was far more than one pair of pyjamas in the tangled heap. Unravelling the clothes, I pulled out four pairs of knickers and three sets of bottoms.

A dismal, draining feeling crept across my skin as the memory of another little girl I had cared for broke the surface of my thoughts. Four-year-old Freya came to stay soon after I first registered as a foster carer seven years earlier, along with her younger sister and baby brother. She had a habit of wearing all of her clothes in bed, one layer on top of another. It was her way of trying to keep herself safe, should anyone pay an unwelcome nightly visit to her room, as her father had done.

Feeling nauseous, I stared at Phoebe's fragile back, trying not to let past experience colour my perception. Foster carers, like social workers, can be prone to jumping to conclusions and piling on layers of clothing was not necessarily an indication of abuse; it could simply be yet another manifestation of her condition. 'Phoebe,' I said gently, holding up the smelly clothing. 'Why did you wear so many pairs of pyjamas to bed?'

She stared at me blankly, so I decided not to make an issue of it. Stuffing the clothes into a carrier bag, I dropped it onto the floor. 'Do you mind if I give your hair a wash, Phoebe? I won't do anything else, just your hair. Is that OK?'

'NOOO!' she howled. 'I hate having my hair washed.'

'Yes, I can see that. But you need to have it done.'

My tone made it clear that refusing was not an option. Surprisingly, she sat motionless as I lifted the shower head and dampened her hair down, running my fingers over the stubby ends. It really was frizzy, almost Afro-style in texture. I reached up and unlocked a cabinet fixed up high on the wall and retrieved the shampoo, squeezing a generous blob into my palms. After rinsing the suds away I smoothed in some conditioner, trying to massage it all the way through to her scalp. The tightness of her hair seemed to loosen so I lavished another handful through, rubbing it in with my fingertips.

Phoebe wriggled away, whimpering.

'Keep still or you'll get conditioner in your eyes,' I said. As I massaged and rubbed her scalp, the texture softened beneath my fingers. Strangely, the tendrils seemed to be extending, like the hair of one of those dolls that Emily had years ago, where the style could be altered by winding a ponytail in and out of the head. It was then I realised her hair wasn't as roughly chopped as I had first thought; it was actually matted.

'Owwww!' Phoebe began to howl.

'It's alright, you're done now,' I soothed. I wasn't surprised she'd been moaning – it must have been very uncomfortable. There were still balls of matted hair clumped to her scalp and I was itching to sort them out but I decided to rinse her off and tackle it again next time. Leaving Phoebe to dry herself, I grabbed the bag of soiled clothes and went downstairs to prepare breakfast, wondering why on earth any mother would leave her daughter's hair to get into such a bad state.

Phoebe managed to eat a few mouthfuls of porridge before clanking her spoon onto the table. Leaning forward to rest her elbows, she cupped her chin in her hands and watched the rest of us tuck into our chocolate pancakes with a look of sickly distaste on her face. She really seemed to derive no pleasure from eating, or anything else, come to think of it. Despite her middle-class background she looked malnourished, her cheeks the colour of frozen pastry and her eyes dull and lifeless. She had that look that children seem to get the day before a cold comes out, where their eyes just don't seem right.

After clearing away the breakfast things I packed up my manicure set and hairdressing scissors and told Phoebe we were going to visit a friend of mine who needed some help. The friend was actually an ex-neighbour who was elderly and unable to get out and about as she once did. Apart from one son there was no one else to help her so I paid her a call once a week to give her hair a wash and tidy the house.

Once or twice over the last couple of years I had made the suggestion that her son might consider running some of the errands himself but each time I broached the subject he shuddered, declaring old age made him nauseous.

Today Mary had requested a haircut and foot manicure, something I wasn't looking forward to with any relish, but it was a relief to escape the gloomy confines of the house. Before we left I suggested that Phoebe choose a book to take with her and I was surprised to find what an interest she showed in selecting one. While she scanned our bookshelves there were no strange whirly arm movements or whooping noises; she just ran her fingers across the spines, pulling one out every now and again to examine the cover. I was also a bit taken aback by the one she finally settled on: Roald Dahl's *The Giraffe and the Pelly and Me*. I wasn't sure she'd be able to manage it and was wondering whether she chose it for Quentin Blake's colourful illustrations alone, when she read the blurb out loud, inflecting parts and showing real expression. Amazed, I chastised myself for jumping to conclusions and underestimating her.

With an interest in reading, I hoped that Phoebe would behave and let me get on with sorting Mary out. And I was grateful to find that she did. Apart from exclaiming when we first arrived that the house 'stinks' and that Mary's toenails looked like 'dirty old twigs' she simply sat reading her book and looking up occasionally, watching us with interest. It was a joy to witness her animated face as she read. There were lots of smiles interspersed with gasps and sudden bouts of giggles. I made a mental note to take her to the library so that she could choose from a wider range of books.

Soon after we arrived back home I suggested a walk to the local shop. 'You could have a look around and see if anything takes your fancy for lunch,' I said, hopeful that if I gave Phoebe a small trolley she might gain a bit more enthusiasm for food, the way children often do when they feel involved.

'Hwah.' Phoebe instantly gagged at the thought.

'Alright, not to worry,' I soothed, assuming all the emotion had upset her system. 'I've got to get some milk anyway.'

Jamie looked revolted by the sounds Phoebe was making, watching her with his lip curled in disgust.

It was a lovely spring day with few clouds in the sky. I closed my eyes briefly as Phoebe skipped ahead, tilting my face to the warm sun. The tenseness I was carrying in my shoulders eased slightly as I enjoyed the fresh breeze rippling over my skin. It was such a relief to be out of the house; it had been only half an hour or so, but I felt as if I'd been cooped up for days.

Lowering my face again I saw that Phoebe was spinning her hands either side of her hips and walking with a strange gait, something she hadn't been doing indoors. She began muttering and every so often broke into a snarl, shaking her fist at passing traffic like a confused old drunkard. It really looked most odd and I noticed a few drivers slow down, frowning. One, a young lad driving a white van, did a double take, no doubt surprised to be on the receiving end of aggressive jeers simply for driving inoffensively down the road.

Phoebe reached the mini-store first. To her credit, she obediently waited outside the entrance for me to catch up. Facing the glass doors, she stood with her legs a foot apart, gesticulating wildly at her reflection. Several customers gave her a wide berth as they left the shop, trying to avoid her flaying arms.

As I caught up they stared at me in disapproving puzzlement, as if I'd allowed my eight-year-old daughter access to magic mushrooms or some other hallucinogenic that might explain her strange conduct.

'Come on,' I said, cupping her elbow and guiding her into the shop.

'Ow! Ouch!' she yelled, struggling as if I'd wrestled her into an arm lock. Embarrassed by stares from several other customers, I released my hold, hoping she wouldn't run off. Fortunately her path was blocked by a young woman who rounded the corner from the next aisle, pushing a pram in front of her.

'Ah, a baby!' Phoebe sounded delighted. 'Can I say hello, please?' She leaned into me, her manner suddenly coquettish.

'Yes, nicely then, if that's OK?'

The baby's mother nodded and smiled. 'Of course,' she said, although her expression said otherwise.

'What is its name?' Phoebe asked sweetly, inching a step or two forwards. Without warning she reached into the pram, stroking the newborn's tiny hand.

'*It* is a her,' I said, smiling reassuringly at the new mum, who hovered close by, ready to pounce if necessary.

'Best not to touch the baby,' I warned gently. I was reluctant to set off a tantrum in the busy shop but the look on Phoebe's face prompted me to apply the brakes. Her eyes were swivelling with excitement, but there was also a manic element to her look that frightened me. Despite her slightness, there seemed to be a barely contained violence simmering beneath the surface, an unexploded rage. Besides, I wanted to secure an escape route for the young baby's mother. She looked distinctly uncomfortable and who could blame her?

'It's Ella,' the new mum responded politely, edging herself between Phoebe and the pram.

'Can I kill it?'

The woman looked at me in horror, her eyes widened in alarm. Jerking the pram backwards, she swung it into the next aisle and stalked away, turning to bestow one final look of disgust my way.

'Fucking baby! I'm going to eat it, I am,' Phoebe called out gruffly after her.

'Be quiet,' I growled under my breath, grabbing her elbow again and marching her to the cold aisle so that I could grab some milk. 'You mustn't say horrible things like that.'

'*You mustn't say horrible things like that.*'

I stared at her, considering my best move. 'Right, choose something for lunch and then we'll go,' I suggested mildly, though my teeth were gritted.

'Blwah, ew!' The retching started.

'Right, let's go, right *now*.'

Several heads turned as I slipped my arm around Phoebe's waist, propelling her towards the checkouts. Shoppers from all angles eyed the pair of us as if we carried some contagious disease. An elderly gentleman stood at the end of our aisle, two bags of shopping planted either side of his feet. He stared openly as we approached. Phoebe squirmed and fought me off, still gagging grotesquely. It was an awful, stomach-churning noise and I felt myself reddening with all the attention being focussed on us.

'Goodness, your daughter's clearly out to lunch, my dear,' the old gentleman whispered loudly in the way old people seem to do, his eyes twinkling with sympathy. 'It must be very difficult for you.'

Until fostering I had never realised how rude some people could be. I glanced at Phoebe, wondering the effect such thoughtless words would have on her. Fortunately she seemed to be switching her attention elsewhere. Nodding grimly to the elderly customer, I was about to pay for the milk and guide Phoebe out of the shop when I realised that she had spotted the confectionery shelves.

'Please may I have some chocolate?' she asked, her eloquence incongruous with her unrefined appearance.

Were it not for the fact that she looked as if she might be in danger of snapping in half right there in the middle of the shop, I would have marched her home empty-handed. As it was, I felt desperate to get some calories inside her, in whatever form I could.

'Yes, choose something quickly then,' I told her.

Outside the shop, Phoebe removed the wrapper from her Twix bar, discarding it casually over her shoulder. She was about to tuck into the chocolate when I caught hold of her wrist.

'Wait a minute, honey. Go and pick up your litter and put it in the bin first.'

'You do it.'

'No,' I said calmly. 'It's your wrapper, not mine. You need to pick it up now, before it blows away.'

'No, leave it there. The bin men will get it when they come.' Her tone was dismissive. All at once she shoved a third of the bar in her mouth, her cheeks bulging.

Grabbing the rest of the chocolate from her hand, I held it behind my back. Never one to court attention, I felt conspicuous, uncomfortably aware of the glances we were attracting from passers-by. I forced my shoulders back and tried to compose myself.

'You are not going to eat the chocolate until you deal with the wrapping. By the time I count to five I want you to pick it up and put it where it belongs – in the bin. If you don't do as I ask, I will throw the chocolate away. Do you understand?'

Dropping her hands to her hips, she splayed her legs to stand her ground, glaring at me. 'I'm not picking it up and you can't make me! Give me my chocolate back.'

'One, t-w-o …' I counted as slowly as I could, willing her to turn and do as I'd asked. A small crowd had gathered outside the shop, watching the showdown with amused interest.

'GIVE ME MY FUCKING CHOCOLATE BACK!' she screamed, her face puce with anger.

As a foster carer, it can sometimes be a challenge to see beyond difficult behaviour and not take it personally, particularly if your own children suffer as a result. Mercifully, with regular mealtimes, a calm environment and a reliable routine in place, most children quickly respond and start to seek out the trusted adult's approval.

When looking after a 'challenging' child, I sometimes find myself recalling previous placements – two-year-old Billy, for example, with his pudgy knees, brown eyes full of mischief and the foulest language I've ever heard. After a few weeks in a house where he wasn't regularly set upon by his sadistic stepfather, the toddler was a delight to be around and began to use words that began with letters other than 'f'.

'Three, f-o-u-r …' Mortified though I was, I couldn't give in to Phoebe's demands any more than I could allow her to drink liquid soap. No child could possibly feel secure if they were allowed to wield power over the adults around them. I felt she needed someone to take control and show her that there were limits, lines that I simply wouldn't allow her to cross. Until she learnt to impose those limits herself, something most children grasped as toddlers, I would have to do it for her. I had to accept that there might be nothing I could do to alleviate the problems associated with autism, but I was determined to help her gain some self-control so that she would feel safe in her own skin.

'Five,' I said quietly, dropping the half-mauled bar into the bin and then bending to pick up the wrapper.

Phoebe balled her fists and threw her head back, wailing a tortured roar of fury.

'Well done, my dear. Good on you!' The old man who had watched us inside the shop shuffled over and patted my arm. 'Old-fashioned discipline, that's what she needs. Shame you didn't do it when she was a toddler but at least you're on the right track now. Let's hope it's not too late.'

Shamed, I gave him a crooked smile and turned towards home, praying the outraged Phoebe would follow me without further protest.

She repeated everything I said for the rest of the day – apart from the time she spent screaming for no discernible reason. By midday Emily and Jamie had lost all trace of humour and decided to seek refuge in the garden. Shutting themselves away in the summerhouse, essentially a shed with curtains, they played cards and board games for the entire afternoon. How I longed to follow them and draw up the barricades behind me. I felt guilty that the placement was spoiling the start of their school holiday but at least they were together and it was probably best they gave Phoebe a wide berth for a few days, in case she took it into her head to lash out at one of them again.

My attempts to engage Phoebe in some sort of constructive play failed. She seemed to lack any imagination, preferring to walk around in circles like a caged animal, talking incessantly. Every now and again she would enter a period of calm, when she would sit and chat like any other eight-year-old girl. Once or twice I broached the subject of the mother and baby in the shop, explaining that if she couldn't say anything nice, it would be best not to say anything at all. She responded with a blank expression, as if the incident had been a figment of my imagination. Sometimes it was as if Phoebe had just emerged from a coma and had no access to old knowledge, even if it was from only a few hours earlier.

At least with her hair now clean and less matted, she looked a bit more 'normal', bordering on pretty actually, when she wasn't flapping her arms in a crazy way. I wondered how she behaved at school and whether she had any friends she could play with. She couldn't seem to sit still, even for a minute. It was as if she had restless leg syndrome that had spread to her whole body (my mum would have called it 'Syvitis Dance'). Whatever the cause, her strange actions were exhausting to watch and my appetite was shot to pieces by the time we sat down for our meal that evening.

Phoebe's eyes bulged when I put her dinner on the table, staring at her plate with such horror that anyone would have thought I'd just unveiled a lamb's head instead of pizza Margherita.

'What's wrong, Phoebe? Don't you like pizza?'

I had tried to find out what she might like to eat during the day, but each time I mentioned food she had gagged. Breakfast had been a small bowl of porridge, Phoebe's untouched pancake polished off by Emily, who hated to see good chocolate going to waste. She had refused lunch so I was keen for her to eat something that evening. I thought I couldn't go wrong with a trusty Italian meal. Every child I had fostered so far had had food issues, but usually it was a case of trying to stop them from gorging themselves until they were sick.

Phoebe pushed her plate away, retching. 'I want porridge,' she choked, her eyes irresistibly glued to the source of her revulsion.

Emily lowered her own pizza slowly to her plate and Jamie screwed up his face, staring at Phoebe in disgust. 'Can you stop her making that noise, Mum?' he asked, his chin tucked close to his chest as if close to throwing up himself.

I whipped Phoebe's plate away, slipping it onto the bookshelf behind me. Her shoulders sagged in relief but she continued to make gagging noises.

'Alright, that's enough, Phoebe. Take some deep breaths – it's gone now. But you must tell me what sort of thing you eat at home, so I can get something you like.'

'I only eat porridge,' she said, her breath coming in short gasps. She was almost in tears. Her eyes were still bulging as if food were somehow a threat to her safety.

'Yes, I know you prefer porridge for breakfast, but what do you like for lunch and dinner?'

'*What do you like for lunch and dinner*?' she mocked, then clamped her hand over her mouth. My concern was suspended by a moment's jubilation. She realises, I thought, she actually knows what she's doing. I wasn't quite sure what the implications were but for some reason I was filled with a sense of optimism.

'I only eat porridge, nothing else. Oh, except chocolate. Anything else makes me …' she retched again, exaggeratedly. 'Blwha, sick.'

Emily and Jamie exchanged disgusted glances.

'Can we leave the table, Mum?' they chorused.

'Yes, OK. You can watch TV while you eat your pizza, if you want,' I said, breaking one of our chief house rules. Usually I was quite strict about eating our meals at the table. It was just about the only time in the day when we had a proper, uninterrupted conversation but if our chat was to be interspersed with Phoebe's throat spasms, I supposed it was worth skipping.

Phoebe sat pinching her bare arm, her eyes staring glassily ahead, while I picked at the rest of my meal. Seemingly oblivious to the red marks forming on her skin, she increased the pressure, twisting and digging away with short, bitten nails. *Just what is going on inside your head?* I wondered, sensing a dark undercurrent.

That night I lay in bed, filled with a sense of impending doom. Phoebe had eaten very little that day, despite all my coaxing. Before she went to bed I had made her another bowl of porridge with a heavy grating of chocolate on top and she had nibbled at it but without any gusto. Could it be possible that porridge was literally all she ever ate?

Still, I thought, trying to focus on the positives, at least Emily and Jamie seemed to be coping well with Phoebe's arrival. There were times when their own lives hadn't been easy; their father and I had separated eight years earlier when they were much younger. I registered as a foster carer soon after my divorce and in a way I think fostering helped ease the transition from a nuclear to a single-parent family. Our house seemed much livelier with lots of children around, even those troubled and withdrawn. Though their dad, who lives less than a mile away from us, was and still is a big part of their lives, Emily and Jamie always missed the chaos that comes with being part of a full family, whenever it was just the three of us at home.

It was the sound of their laughter earlier that had helped me through the gruesomeness of our first full day with Phoebe. I felt so proud of them: not only were they kind and loving, they possessed a wonderful ability to laugh at the downright awful, a gift inherited from their father. Somehow, remembering their capacity for humour helped me in marshalling my own and my low mood slowly lifted.

But it wasn't just fretting over Phoebe's starvation diet that was keeping me awake: knots in my stomach reminded me that I had to supervise a contact session between Phoebe and her parents in the morning. When children are removed without parental consent, contact usually takes place under the supervision of contact workers employed by the local authority, but since Phoebe was in voluntary care, the arrangement was to be more flexible.

Curious as I was to find out what her parents were like, contact was one of the tasks of fostering that I dreaded. Looking after the children was often the easy bit; Looked After Children (LAC) reviews, Child Protection

Conferences and contact sessions, in fact anything involving other adults was the unappealing side of the job as far as I was concerned. Being a natural introvert, I tended to shy away from meetings, particularly when there was the possibility of confrontation.

Turning to my side, I tuned in to the low hum of traffic drifting through my open bedroom window, trying to dismiss thoughts of Phoebe from my mind.

Chapter 6

The smart-looking couple stood a few feet inside the entrance of La Trattoria, their shoulders turned fractionally away from each other, expressions downturned. When he spotted us, the man, in his early 40s and tall, stepped forward with a confident air. Phoebe bounded ahead of us and ran to his outstretched arms, throwing her thin arms around his neck.

'How have you been, my little sweetheart?' Robin Steadman asked, smiling warmly as he lifted his daughter from the ground and tickled her side. She squealed with excitement. Slim but broad-shouldered, he looked immaculate in his double-breasted suit and tie, every inch the man about town. Salt and pepper, wavy hair was swept back from his tanned face; it was easy to imagine him sitting behind a shiny desk in a suave London bond broker's office.

Phillipa, Phoebe's mother, lingered behind: although clearly younger than her husband, she looked tired, concern etched onto her features. While Robin gave the impression he had just returned from some exotic holiday in Dubai, his wife looked as if this was her first venture into the sunshine for several months. Her skin appeared washed out and she gave off an anguished air. It seemed that Robin was coping with the sudden separation from his daughter with more ease than Phillipa.

'Hello, darling,' she said in lady-like, reedy tones, once Phoebe had released her grip on her father. I wasn't sure if it was just her middle-class accent but her voice sounded brittle to me, lacking in any warmth.

'*Hello, darling*,' Phoebe repeated, rebuffing her mother's attempt to cuddle up to her. Phillipa's lips drew into a tight line. So, you find her parrot behaviour infuriating too, I thought, noticing the flash of irritation in her expertly kohl-lined eyes.

As Robin shook my hand the cuff of his shirt shifted, revealing an expensive watch on his wrist. 'Shall we?' he asked in an impressive, well-educated accent, gesturing to a nearby table. He smiled charmingly as he pulled out a chair for me to sit down. Waving Emily and Jamie along to the opposite end of the table, I seated myself between my children and the temporarily reunited family. It was close enough to monitor their conversation but far enough away to allow them a little privacy too.

Glancing around, I was grateful to see that the place was near-empty, in case the smell of pizza should set off Phoebe's gagging again. Jamie scanned the drinks menu. Emily feigned an interest but every so often she took a surreptitious peep sideways, eyeing Phoebe's parents. At 14, Emily was old enough to stay at home but had asked to come along. I think she was as curious to meet them as I was.

Once we were settled in our seats, Robin lifted his hand and seconds later a waiter appeared. Phoebe cuddled up to her father, bouncing up and down so that her head kept bumping into his chin. 'Careful, darling.' She ignored him, continuing to bob furiously and squealing loudly. Patiently, he craned his neck, ordering drinks over the top of her head.

Phillipa, by contrast, was perched nervously on the edge of the seat opposite Phoebe, her hands twisting a napkin. Expensively coiffured, with high cheekbones and thickly lashed blue eyes, she made me feel a bit scruffy in her presence and I began flattening down my disobedient hair. She should have been beautiful and yet an air of coldness shaded any radiance from shining through. She glanced towards me then quickly looked away, smiling towards her daughter. 'So, what have you been up to, darling? Have you been keeping busy at Rosie's?' I got the feeling she made the enquiry because it was expected of her, rather than out of genuine interest. There was definitely a distance there.

'*Been keeping busy at Rosie's?*'

An uncomfortable silence followed Phoebe's mocking of her mother, eventually broken by a self-assured Robin. 'I bet you've been – the most …' I couldn't make out the entire sentence because the pair were snuggled so closely together, him whispering affectionately into her ear. Every now and again her bony hand rose up, touching her father's cheek. It was as if Phillipa's presence was superfluous to both father and daughter. Clearly, I wasn't the only one to notice.

Phillipa lowered her gaze, looking ill at ease. I felt instant pity for her. Leaning across the table, I decided to try and engage her in conversation, an effort to ease her discomfort.

'Do you mind if I ask you a few things, Phillipa?'

She shook her head. 'Not at all.'

'What does Phoebe like to eat? The only thing I can tempt her with is porridge.'

Phillipa reddened. 'She's fixated on cereal at the moment, I'm afraid. Becoming fanatical about certain things can be one of the effects of autism.' She seemed to shudder when she mentioned her daughter's condition. It was strange, really – she was so articulate that I should have been the one who felt intimidated and yet it was she who appeared flustered.

Embarrassed to delve into issues of hygiene with someone so refined but feeling obliged to investigate, I asked her why Phoebe's hair was matted.

She didn't directly look at me as she answered. 'She hates water so we try and get bathtime over with as quickly as possible. I'm afraid she's been even more obsessive about it lately – she just won't allow me anywhere near her hair.'

At that moment Phoebe lunged across the table, catching her mother's face with her fingernails. 'Shut up,' she screeched, 'stop talking about me!'

Phillipa flinched, glancing around the restaurant with embarrassment. How difficult it must be, I thought, to have every outing ruled by someone so unpredictable. It would hardly be surprising if their marriage were under strain. Even so, they did seem to indulge rather than control Phoebe's spoilt behaviour. Were they really that frightened of their own daughter's tantrums that they couldn't even persuade her to wash her hair? Robin lowered flattened hands through the air in front of his daughter, trying to placate her. 'It's alright, Phoebe. Mummy's not going to talk about you any more.' He had a rich, deep voice that would have been perfect for radio. 'Ah, here we are, sweetheart,' he said, as a hesitant-looking waiter lowered a tray of drinks on the table.

Phoebe peppered the next hour with outlandish actions and loud screeches. Phillipa sat meekly, watching as her unruffled husband tried to cajole his out-of-control daughter into calming down. Robin remained remarkably cool throughout, making no attempt to restrain her, even when she lashed out at her mother again. I found myself getting more and more wound up as I watched them let their child walk all over them.

Apart from a few monosyllabic replies from Emily and Jamie in response to my attempts at conversation, they spent most of the time in silence, avidly watching the interaction between Phoebe and her parents. As 11 o'clock approached, Phillipa made a show of checking her watch as if trying to remind me to call time on their session. I wondered how she managed to get through whole days in the company of Phoebe, if she found just an hour so torturous.

When Robin signalled that we were ready to leave the waiter quickly returned with two separate bills, no doubt relieved that our noisy party would be gone before the lunchtime trade arrived.

Robin swept the receipts across the table with his well-groomed, long fingers. 'They're for you, I believe.'

'Oh, thanks.' I took the bill for Emily and Jamie's drinks, handing the other back to him. 'If you go to the civic centre, you can claim it all back there.' I knew from experience that social services covered the cost of contact in the community, with no apparent limit. If Phoebe's parents had chosen to take her to the cinema or the theatre, the money would be diverted from already overstretched budgets to pay for the trip. In the past I had found the idea galling, particularly when the children had been removed as a result of severe abuse. I couldn't help but feel that feckless parents were being rewarded for their appalling behaviour. Surely you can afford to pay for your daughter's own milkshake? I thought acerbically.

'No.' His mouth twisted in annoyance. Phoebe stiffened. His wife eyed him warily as he tapped the bill with his forefinger. 'My daughter has been removed for no good reason. I have to be supervised by strangers if I want to spend an hour with her.' An edge crept into his smooth voice. 'Do you really think I'm going to cover the cost of that sort of humiliation?'

From nowhere, an image of Phoebe's tangled pyjama bottoms flashed into my thoughts. The memory gave me a disquieting feeling. Could it be that she had suffered abuse at the hands of this man? I banished the thought, telling myself it was natural for him to feel resentful, when his only daughter, and perhaps most treasured possession, had been snatched away from him.

My own children dropped their straws, watching us keenly. Jamie looked about ready to pounce. My son was a simple soul, without an aggressive bone in his body, but he was always particularly protective of me. I smiled at both of them to convey the message that all was well. Then all at once something in Robin's eyes flickered and there was another change in pitch. I think he must have realised the effect his tone was having on me because his frown softened. 'I would prefer you dealt with it now,' he smiled amiably, 'if you wouldn't mind.'

Conciliatory, I shook my head. 'Not a problem,' I said, springing to my feet in my customary wish to oblige. Grabbing the tab, I slung my bag over my shoulder and went to the till. As I entered my pin number into the credit card reader I glanced across at Phillipa. She hovered behind her husband as he held Phoebe's hands, supporting her while she jumped up and down on his highly polished, shiny black shoes.

As we said our goodbyes there was no trace of bad feeling between us. Robin shook my hand again and thanked me warmly. There was no real reason, then, for the surge of angst rising in my chest. Except that beneath his charming exterior I was beginning to suspect Phoebe's father might be concealing something all the more disturbing.

Chapter 7

The journey back was stressful, with Phoebe parroting everything Jamie said.

'Mum, please stop her,' he groaned, drawing his hands roughly down his face and twisting his lip with agitation.

Phoebe was delighted by his distress.

'*Mum, please stop her*.'

'That's enough, Phoebe. You'll go to your room when we get home if you don't stop,' I said firmly, regretting the words as soon as I'd said them. Having recently attended a Behaviour Management course, I was aware that threatening to send a child to their room was frowned upon. Apparently it gave the impression that bedtime was a punishment. Any child who had been sexually abused would already harbour negative feelings around night-time and foster carers were supposed to overlook bad behaviour where possible, rewarding good behaviour instead.

Positive praise was all very well in theory, I had found, but in the first few weeks of placement often there was precious little that could be applauded. Of course, most children responded well to praise, but being unable to impose some form of penalty made fostering that much harder. Ignoring bad behaviour didn't always help it to go away.

As we neared home I decided to pop in to see my mother. She'd only met Phoebe briefly when she came to pick Emily and Jamie up a few days previously, and she was eager to get to know her. During our daily telephone conversations I had regaled her with our struggles so far but I think she thought I had embellished the tales for her entertainment.

When Mum opened the door she greeted us with her usual warm embrace, though rather than wrapping her arms around Phoebe she patted her on the arm, giving it a friendly squeeze.

'Oh goodness, you're all skin and bone, girl!'

Phoebe stiffened, staring at her arm as if Mum had rubbed her over with hot coals. If Mum noticed her reaction (which I'm sure she had, as nothing much got past her), she ignored it. I was touched by her ability to welcome the tribes of children I thrust upon her. Over the years she had treated them with as much generosity as she had shown her own grandchildren, something she didn't have to do.

'Lovely to see you all – enjoying being off school, are you?' Cheerfully ushering us all into her cosy living room, Mum launched into her standard routine of listing all the sweet and savoury items available in the kitchen.

Emily and Jamie dived in, grabbed some goodies and then planted themselves firmly on her sofa. They were so comfortable at their grandmother's house that it was like a second home to them. Phoebe hovered behind me; I could see she felt a bit uncomfortable.

'Come on, love, don't be shy. Have a chocolate cookie or something. I made 'em fresh this morning.'

Oh dear, I thought, I should have mentioned to Mum about Phoebe's food issues. Talk of freshly baked biscuits and the like was bound to set off her retching. But I was wrong. Amazingly, Phoebe smiled shyly as she took Mum's hand, allowing herself to be guided to an armchair, where she reached out and accepted one of the warm offerings. Although Mum could sometimes be a force to be reckoned with she was naturally kind, a throwback to a gentler age. It was something I think Phoebe could sense.

With the children within earshot our conversation revolved mainly around the latest family gossip, the comings and goings of Mum's new neighbours and the latest developments on *Emmerdale*.

'Oh, and I forgot to tell you what your brother got up to last week.'

'*Oh, and I forgot to tell you what your brother got up to last week.*'

I smiled wryly to myself: Phoebe was definitely feeling at home. Mum stared at her with one of her frighteningly stern looks, the type, I'm ashamed to say, which still had a shrinking effect on me. Phoebe looked away.

After a moment, Mum continued: 'Where was I? Oh yes, Chris. He's only gone and …'

'He's only gone and …'

'Don't interrupt adults,' Mum snapped. 'It's rude.'

'Fuck off, whore!'

Mum's jaw dropped about two inches. Emily and Jamie spun around, astonished anyone would dare speak to their grandmother in that way. If Mum hadn't recovered quickly and said, 'Wash your mouth out with soap,' I would have laughed at their reaction.

I cringed. 'It's alright, Phoebe, she doesn't mean it.' And to Mum I growled through gritted teeth, 'You mustn't say things like that – you'll get me struck off.' What did she think she was doing?

'Send them social workers around here and I'll give them short shrift.' Mum waggled her finger at Phoebe. 'She's the one coming into my house with the filthy mouth.'

Despite our close relationship there were days when my mother was capable of driving me nuts. Did she not realise the trouble she could get me in for saying such a thing? I remembered another foster carer telling me that she had a baby removed from her care because during a visit from her supervising social worker, her own mother, who had offered to change the baby's nappy, exclaimed, 'Ooh, look at that lovely bottom! Don't you just want to eat it?'

Horrified, the social worker had stared at the foster carer as if she'd been raised by cannibals. She was reinstated soon after the investigation was completed but the baby had gone through an unnecessary move and the foster carer had almost given up her vocation through the stress of it all.

I suppose I should have been grateful that Mum hadn't threatened to 'cut her tongue out' as she often did when my brothers were young and repeated something they'd heard in the playground.

Mum was still staring at me belligerently. No surprise there, but what did amaze me was Phoebe's reaction to the whole exchange. Her eyes were filled with amusement as she stared at both of us and then, to my surprise, she began laughing.

We stayed another hour before travelling the short journey home. As I drove, I churned Phoebe's reaction over in my mind. I had thought that autism affected a person's ability to appreciate humour since sufferers generally took everything anyone said in the literal sense, but if that were the case, Phoebe would surely have been horrified by Mum's 'threat' to wash her mouth out with soap?

It was yet another anomaly to puzzle over.

When we got home Emily invited Phoebe to sit at the table and do some colouring, freeing me to prepare lunch. I was amazed by my daughter's fortitude – Phoebe had aggravated both of my children since first light so it was a credit to Emily's levels of tolerance that she was even prepared to share the same floor space – but I asked Phoebe to go and sit at the top of the stairs for five minutes instead, as penance for winding Jamie up in the car by repeating everything he had said.

As we sat down to eat he was subdued. I couldn't help but smile to myself as he slipped past a sullen Phoebe, taking a seat at the opposite end of the table. He glanced sideways to make sure she was at a safe distance, wary of getting a wet finger rammed into his ear again.

'I hate the way you make porridge,' Phoebe said as she swept her bowl away, arching back in her chair. Her ribs were visible through her T-shirt. 'I'm not going to eat it.'

Extremely jittery, I got the feeling it was an effort for her to sit at the table, like she wanted to spring up and spin around the house.

'That's a shame,' I said, non-committal, determined not to be drawn into a battle.

'*That's a shame*.'

There was a pause. Nonchalantly, I took a bite of my sandwich.

'I mean it. I'm not even going to taste it.'

'Yes, I heard you, Phoebe. Now, let's decide what to do tomorrow. We could go ice-skating or maybe hire some bikes and go for a ride.'

'I've got to revise, Mum.' Emily was studying for her GCSEs and so it would be good for her to have the house to herself for a whole day.

Jamie shrugged his shoulders, eyeing Phoebe. A keen sportsman, he usually jumped at the opportunity of an action-packed day out. I guessed that his reticence was probably fuelled by the idea of another disastrous car ride with our new interloper.

Furious that I was showing no interest in her hunger strike, Phoebe glared at me, drumming her fingers on the table. Writhing in her seat, she stirred her porridge round and round, then spun both hands around, hurling porridge through the air. It was then that I decided to stop pandering to her autism and treat her just as I would any other child.

'Stop that right now,' I insisted, wondering whether she was so manic because seeing her parents had made her feel extra homesick. Whatever the reason, I knew that being lenient wasn't going to help.

'*Stop that right now*.' A glimmer in her eyes told me she understood exactly how infuriating her parroting behaviour was. I knew she couldn't help it – her autism controlled her, not the other way around – but I couldn't help but feel she was enjoying the effects of it too. Observing contact between Phoebe and her parents had been a telling experience. It was clear that she was allowed to rule the roost at home, with few boundaries in place. Watching her spinning her arms around, I realised that she was also dominating all of us too. I made a mental note to record the interactions with her parents in my daily diary. Regular records might help to paint an overall picture of their relationship.

'Phoebe, if you don't stop what you're doing, I will have to make you stop.'

All at once Phoebe picked up her porridge, throwing it across the table with a screech of delight. The edge of the bowl caught Jamie on the chest, the contents spattering all over the table and into his lap. With a loud crash, the china met the floor, cracking into several jagged pieces. Jamie clapped his hands to his chest, his face reddening with alarm.

'Can I eat in my room, Mum?'

My heart went out to him but I didn't want him to sit in his room when he had done nothing wrong. 'No, Jamie, you stay where you are.' Grabbing a tea towel, I mopped up around him, determined not to let Phoebe sabotage our time together as a family. Tempted to yell at her, I held my breath, counting backwards from 10 to one. The urge subdued, I spoke with calm firmness, 'Phoebe, I have asked you not to throw things. It's dangerous and could hurt someone very badly. I'd like you to leave the table, please.'

With a look of delight, Phoebe scooted off to the sofa, where she sat with her legs clasped to her chest, rocking manically back and forth. Jamie's shoulders visibly dropped and he picked up his fork, tucking into his lunch with relief. Annoyed that Phoebe had achieved what she'd wanted but determined not to spoil the rest of our meal, I chattered about where we should visit over the next few days, the weather – anything to try and lift the gloom Phoebe had left in her wake.

'So,' I said cheerfully, 'what's on the menu for this evening, Ems?' Once a week Emily cooked an evening meal for the family and really went to town, setting the table with candles, embroidered placemats and napkins.

Emily opened her mouth to speak but Jamie butted in. 'I wouldn't mind having dinner on my lap again,' he said drily, raising his eyebrows and staring down at his porridge-splattered trousers.

Emily roared with laughter. I chuckled, burying my head in my hands. It was the first spontaneous laugh the three of us had shared since her arrival. The morose atmosphere lightened in an instant. Thank goodness for a sense of humour, I thought.

Emily offered to wash up while I cleared the table. I was about to make a pile of the plates when I heard Emily gasp. Expecting to find Phoebe nibbling the remote, I spun around, shocked to see her half-inclined on the sofa, legs spread wide, with her jeans hanging at her ankles. With a look of frenzy on her face, she was panting and holding her knickers aside, trying to manoeuvre a pen inside the elastic. She looked like a young actress in a horror movie, the whites of her eyes on full display again. Emily was rooted to the spot, staring at the scene with her mouth gaping.

'Upstairs now!' I snapped at Jamie. I wasn't sure if he'd seen what I had but I was praying his view had been blocked. His eyes filled with tears. Throwing back his chair, he gave me a wounded look and headed for the stairs.

'Phoebe, don't be so gross,' Emily said, mortified.

Putting a finger to my lips, I signalled for Emily to be quiet. One of the challenges of being a foster carer was learning to deal with shocking or taboo issues in a balanced, rational way. I still find it hugely shocking to witness a young child behaving in a sexualised way but I knew from experience that it would be wrong to express our disgust, possibly exacerbating the child's long-term psychological problems.

'*Phoebe, don't be so gross*.' I was grateful to see her sit up, a strange smirk on her face.

'Emily, would you go up to Jamie? Phoebe, if you want to touch yourself, you need to go to your room and do it in private. But you mustn't ever use a pen to do it, or anything else. You could really hurt yourself.' I felt my cheeks flushing as I spoke. 'I don't want to see you doing that ever again, do you understand me?'

Expecting to be mimicked, I was surprised when she gave me a look of bemusement.

'Why not?' she asked, simply.

How could I explain such a taboo subject to a child with obvious learning difficulties? Her blank expression told me that she wasn't remotely fazed by what she had done, or the effect it had on everyone around her. She literally had no idea that there was anything offensive or unusual about her behaviour.

'No one wants to see you do that and I don't want you to hurt yourself.' *It makes me feel sick to my stomach*, I wanted to tell her but decided it would be wise to delay any further discussion until I had given the situation more thought. Instead I said, 'Now, would you like to watch television?'

There was no plateau, when caring for Phoebe. At the end of an exhausting day when all I wanted to do was get through the mission of dinner, bath and bed so that I could enter a 'nothingness' zone, Phoebe would crank things up a level. That evening I sat beside her in the upstairs hallway, reading the next chapter of *The Giraffe and the Pelly and Me*, sincerely hoping that she had reached a ceiling and there would be no more shocks in store.

Every now and again Phoebe leaned sideways to examine the pictures, her head brushing my shoulder. I wasn't sure if it was her way of asking for affection but I took the opportunity anyway, reaching out to stroke her head. She jerked away.

'Don't do that – I hate you.'

Reading bedtime stories was often the highlight of my day as a foster carer. With many of my placements, I was the first person ever to have read to the child before they went to sleep. It's funny how quickly children embrace story time as part of a regular routine to help them unwind. Usually I enjoyed it as much as they did, particularly as it marked the end of my working day.

Story time with Phoebe was a whole different experience. Before I had finished one sentence she started repeating me so that by the end of the last page my head was throbbing and my patience running thin.

'Again!' she shouted, as I snapped the book shut. I was amazed she had enjoyed it but my nerves were by then so frayed that I couldn't face another chapter.

'Not tonight – bedtime now but we'll read again in the morning if you'd like, as long as you don't say anything unkind. If you do, I'll stop reading straight away, OK?'

She looked at me quizzically but didn't answer. Could she even remember saying she hated me? I told her to change into her pyjamas and left her to get undressed, hoping she would digest what I'd said. After a few moments I leaned my head around the door.

'Goodnight, Phoebe.'

'*Goodnight, Phoebe.*'

Emily and Jamie were on the sofa when I returned to the living room and flopped between them with a loud sigh. 'Fancy a game of rummy?' I asked. Jamie nodded, fishing out his pack of cards from the magazine rack. After a full day with Phoebe it was the last thing I wanted to do, but a bit of individual time with the children usually worked wonders, relieving the tension that flowed between us in the early days of a placement.

Jamie sat opposite, shuffling the cards.

'She's so weird,' he said bluntly.

'Shush, Jamie. Keep your voice down.' I knew that children in care seemed to have an eerie bat-like ability to hear through walls, a response to being kept in the dark about so many issues concerning them. 'We don't want to hurt her feelings.'

He looked chastened, drawing invisible patterns on the joker at the top of the pack. 'Sorry, but I don't think she *has* any feelings. She's not very nice – I thought she was supposed to be warm and friendly?'

'Mmm, bit of a stretch of the imagination, I must admit. But maybe that's because we don't understand her yet.' I looked at Emily. 'What do you think, Em?'

My daughter gave me a sidelong glance. 'What she did to my butterflies wasn't too friendly,' she jibed, grinning.

'And chucking plates isn't that warm,' Jamie cut in, his eyes twinkling with humour.

I laughed out loud, throwing my arms around both of them and planting kisses on their heads. 'You're wonderful, both of you, do you know that?'

When my two went off to bed I settled myself in front of the computer, cradling a cup of hot tea in my hands. Sipping at my drink, I thought for a moment, then typed 'autism', 'masturbation', 'young girls' into Google's search box. I was about to click the SEARCH button when the colour drained from my face as I realised what sort of results might come back. Half-choking on my tea I fumbled for the backspace button, hurriedly deleting all trace of what I'd written. Safely faced with a blank screen again I slumped back in the chair, filled with relief.

Whatever was I thinking? Drawing my hands down my face, I cursed my own stupidity. I had known a few foster carers whose electronic equipment had been confiscated as a result of allegations made. Phones, laptops and PCs were then analysed by police officers, searching for inappropriate content. Frustrated, I realised I would have to conduct research in the old-fashioned way and visit the library.

Savouring the warmth from the cup as it seeped into my fingers, I allowed my thoughts to drift. Toying with the mouse and watching the cursor dance around the screen, I decided to take a different approach and entered 'symptoms of autism' into the search engine, opting for the NHS choice at the top of the page. It was as though the author of the webpage had spent a day analysing Phoebe and listing his conclusions: unable to reciprocate in relationships, dislike of others, struggling with friendships, difficulty understanding personal space and recognising other people's feelings, refusing overtures of affection, repeating words or phrases over and over, strange facial or body movements such as spinning or flapping hands, unusual sleeping or eating habits.

But there was no mention of sexualised behaviour.

Before logging off I sent Lenke an email with a copy of my daily log, detailing the 'pen' incident. Any disturbing conduct needed to be carefully recorded and I hoped that by reporting it, I could purge the image from my mind.

But it wasn't going to be that simple.

I tossed and turned in bed, worrying about the implications of Phoebe's self-abuse and wondering whether to try and discuss it with her, or if the matter was best ignored. I felt sad that a child would treat their own body in such a degrading way, though it seemed that Phoebe had no understanding of what she was actually doing. She might not, I thought, but my own children did. Could it possibly be reasonable to expose an 11-year-old boy to the kind of behaviour Phoebe had exhibited? And what effect might it have on his developing mind?

I pulled the duvet up around my chin but still I couldn't get comfortable, feeling stifled instead of cocooned. When I registered as a foster carer, I had resolved never to reject a child when the going got tough. If I asked for Phoebe to be moved on, I would be letting myself down, as well as her. What effect might outright rejection have on her? I wondered. But, on the other hand, my first responsibility had to be for Emily and Jamie.

Over the years they had witnessed children struggling with all sorts of issues, responding with patience and kindness. I knew they would probably never ask for Phoebe to leave; they were too sympathetic to her plight to do that. But having to live with a child with such severe problems – my sleep-deprived brain worried that was a bit too much to expect them to cope with.

As dawn approached, I decided I had no choice but to do something about it.

Chapter 8

It was with a heavy heart that I came downstairs the next morning, Phoebe following closely behind. She was unusually reserved, as if she could sense my plans to end the placement. Jamie was already in the kitchen, hair dishevelled, spilt cereal grains and pools of milk all over the worktop where he'd prepared his own breakfast. 'Hi, Mum,' he chirped mid-chew, wiping his mouth on his sleeve. 'Morning, Phoebe,' he added as an afterthought.

'Morning, Jamie.'

We both stared at her, mouths agape. Jamie eyed me warily as he bent to tie the laces of his trainers, confused by her 'normal' response. She seemed oblivious to our surprise, absently studying the side panel of Jamie's discarded cereal box.

'I'm going to practise on my skateboard, Mum,' Jamie told me, still watching Phoebe suspiciously.

'OK.'

Perhaps sensing the dip in my spirits, he straightened, stretching an arm around my shoulder. 'Alright, Mum?'

'Course I am.' I squeezed him for a bit longer than usual and he drew back, studying me closely.

'Sure?'

Briskly, I brushed some toast crumbs from his top. 'Of course – go on, off you go.'

'Can I come and watch you, Jamie?' Phoebe asked sweetly.

'S'pose so,' he answered hesitantly. He seemed as baffled by her metamorphosis as I was. I wondered what could possibly have evoked such a puzzling transformation. Last night she had put on a shockingly disturbed display and yet today she seemed no different to any other eight-year-old. That was the puzzling thing about Phoebe; there seemed to be no clear pattern to her behaviour and no discernible triggers. It was almost as if she had the power to switch to autistic mode when the mood suited.

Phoebe skipped past him and slipped her shoes on. Jamie frowned as he followed her into the garden, shaking his head.

Jamie's bewilderment was almost comical but did nothing to lift my mood as I reached for the telephone and dialled Desmond's mobile. Waiting for the call to connect I drew a deep breath, wondering how he would react when I told him that the placement wasn't working out. Giving up on a child went against the grain and I felt awful about it but I had to consider the needs of Emily and Jamie, as well as Phoebe's own welfare.

I sighed with relief when the call switched to a recorded message, allowing me a short reprieve before I disgraced myself. In guilty, lowered tones I left my message: 'Hi, Des, we need to talk. Could you call me?' Giving up on a placement was generally frowned on by social workers and I had never done it before.

After making a cup of coffee I sat at the dining table, watching my phone as if it was an unexploded bomb. A warm breeze floated through a gap in the patio doors, the clear blue sky promising a nice day ahead. Staring into the garden, I knew I should make some plans to take the children somewhere, but part of me was reluctant to venture out for fear of alarming the locals again.

Anyway, Jamie seemed to be enjoying himself. He sped along the garden path with characteristic boundless energy, apparently unscathed by what he had witnessed the previous day. A slight movement from behind him caught my attention. Nestled between trellis borders on our decking area at the bottom of the garden, Phoebe sat on the patio swing, her forlorn figure framed by the purple wisteria that had wound itself around the frame. My guilt resurfaced with a vengeance as I watched her rocking gently back and forth, one thin leg dangling, the other tucked beneath her slight body. If only I could help her without risking the sanity of my own children, I thought.

My mind began to drift. I remembered young Alfie again; a boy who had spent much of the first three years of his life locked up in his filthy bedroom while his addict mother earned her drug money by selling her body, just a few feet from his own door. Initially withdrawn, he spent weeks lashing out, spitting and kicking whenever we approached him.

I remember with clarity one particular day, early on in the placement back in 2005. Alfie's temper had declined into meltdown over some perceived injustice and he sank his teeth into my neck, his jaws clamping me in an agonising bite. In that moment I was convinced there was nothing I could do to help him and was about ready to make the 'I can't cope' call dreaded by foster carers up and down the country. It was only a strong reluctance to give up on him that kept me going. If I'm honest, I had no idea if what I was doing for Alfie was right, but somehow, simple caring had made a difference. He had seemed fractured when he came to us, broken and depressed. When he moved on nine months later it was as a robust, energetic little boy and I was immensely glad I had seen it through.

Emily and Jamie often talked of him, remembering the time he spent with us fondly. Memories of Alfie gave me strength. I had entered into fostering in the hope of providing a safe haven from the harshness of the world; it felt terrible to think that in this case I might be adding to rather than easing a child's suffering. Maybe there was a way of getting through this? I silently wondered.

The phone rang, interrupting my thoughts. It was Phoebe's social worker.

'Did you get my email, Lenke?'

'Yes, this does seem a bit disturbing behaviour, yes.' She sounded harassed, impatient. 'I have to make the statutory visit within the next week anyway. We could discuss it then, yes?'

'It doesn't *seem* disturbing, it *is* disturbing – do you think we should start the ball rolling with CAMHS now?' While I appreciated that Phoebe's main problems stemmed from her autism, I thought it might help to seek some professional advice from the Child and Adolescent Mental Health Services, particularly as she might soon be moving on from me. They could support her through the move and would also be able to discern whether counselling would be of any benefit to her and her parents. From experience I knew it could take several weeks to get an appointment arranged.

'No, I see no need for that at all. Phoebe is a great mimicker, yes? She has probably seen something on a music video or film, perhaps.'

The social worker spoke with a tone of finality, clearly looking for a convenient pause in which to end the conversation, whereas I was only just getting started.

'I don't think so,' I scoffed. 'I've seen some risqué things on MTV but I've never known anyone to do *that*.' Not even Rihanna, I thought, caustically.

Lenke sighed as if she'd repeated herself several times already. 'Children with autism, they have difficulty learning the correct boundaries. The testosterone-suppressing medication was considered for Phoebe but there are too many side effects so it was decided not to go ahead with it.'

Before I had a chance to process this new information she was withdrawing, suggesting we meet 'in the next week or so' to discuss matters further. It was as if we were arranging to meet up to discuss soft furnishings. Frustrated by my cowardice at broaching the subject of moving Phoebe on, I ended the call and dropped the handset onto the table.

Never before had I felt as if I were floundering, with no idea what to do for the best. I knew that social awareness in children with autism was impaired but for Lenke to brush Phoebe's actions off so lightly struck me as a cop-out. It also struck me as odd that, although well-seasoned social workers were practically immune to shock, she'd failed to sound as surprised by the pen incident as she might have.

I was about to pull the vacuum cleaner from the cupboard under the stairs when a sudden outbreak of noise drew me hurriedly to the kitchen. With my heart in my throat I threw open the patio doors, wondering what disaster had befallen Phoebe in the few minutes I hadn't been watching her.

Blinking uncomprehendingly, I stood and stared at the scene unfolding in the garden. Jamie must have tied the skateboard to his bike because Phoebe was now riding along the path, towing my cheering son along behind. They both crashed into our heavy border of bushes and landed back on the grass, shrieking with laughter.

Half an hour later they tumbled through the open door, faces flushed, eyes bright. In high spirits they kicked off their shoes in the kitchen and charged into the living room.

'Mum, can we play tennis on the Wii?' Jamie asked.

'Of course,' I answered, staggered by this new development. Phoebe was rosy-cheeked, her whole face shining; I could barely contain my delight. 'You'll have to come off in half an hour or so, though, because Desmond is coming to see us.'

'Yeah!' Jamie loved visits from our social worker. In his younger days, before entering the field of social services, Desmond had spent some time in the US, making his living as a bit-part actor, though from the stories with which he regales us and some of Emily's research on YouTube, it seems he was best known for his role in car-lot commercials. Besides having the most rubbery, expressive face I have ever seen, Des was a talented impressionist and regularly had us all in stitches. He was in the perfect job as far as I was concerned: a real live children's entertainer.

'What's wrong, Phoebe?' I noticed her standing frozen, knuckles white from gripping the Wii controller so tightly.

'Who is Desmond?'

'Our social worker – nothing to worry about, honey. He's a lovely man, isn't he, Jamie?'

'Sure, he's cool.'

'What colour hair does he have?' Her face was contorted, all trace of colour gone.

I considered for a moment, watching as she folded her arms and squeezed them with wringing fingers. Her chest puffed out as if she was holding her breath.

'Erm, dark, I would say. Why?'

Her shoulders dropped at least an inch and she started breathing again, returning her attention to the television.

An unpleasant, creeping feeling returned to my stomach.

'Why did you want to know what colour hair he has, Phoebe?'

She just shrugged.

As the day wore on my anxiety about Phoebe's strange reaction grew. Desmond, who had been delayed by a teenage runaway, didn't make it to us until about 4pm, just as we arrived back from the park. It had been a positive venture out, if only for the fact that we were all adjusting to Phoebe's sudden outbursts and becoming adept at squeezing in our conversations between prolonged bouts of screaming.

'Hello, Phoebe,' Desmond said, holding out his hand for Phoebe to shake. I watched her reaction closely. She stood swaying from side to side with her hands hidden behind her back, eyeing him warily. 'Come on, girl, I don't bite.'

Des's face was just a bit too rugged to be classed as handsome but with his wayward, dark curly hair and deep dimples, he definitely had an appeal. From the moment we met it felt as if we were close friends and so the usual politeness of colleagues was quickly dropped. Clearly Phoebe felt the same. Out of character, she took a step forward and offered up her own thin hand.

Immediately Des whipped his hand away. Stretching his fingers to make a fan, he twisted it on his nose. 'Na na na-na NA!'

Phoebe giggled, watching him expectantly.

Jamie jumped up. 'Hi, Des.'

'Ah, young man – hello again.' Des stretched out his hand and Jamie lunged for it, grabbing before he could pull away. As he shook it a loud farting noise filled the room, courtesy of one of the props Des kept in his pockets. Jamie fell about laughing and Phoebe joined in, screeching loudly.

It was then that the missile came out of nowhere, catching me right in the sensitive area at the side of my head, just above my ear. It hit me with such force that I almost lost my footing and Des lunged forwards, slipping a supportive hand under my arm to steady me. Momentarily dazed, I raised a shaky hand to my head then took in the shards of black plastic covering the floor. Jamie's Wii remote lay in pieces all over the room, shattered after being thrown by Phoebe.

She stared at me triumphantly, apparently delighted by how unyielding my skull appeared to be. Still dazed, I couldn't respond for a moment so I was grateful when Des whisked her away into the kitchen. I could hear him giving her a bit of a lecture as Jamie draped his arm around me. 'Are you alright, Mum?'

Bless him, I thought. I could hear the anger in his voice but I was pleased that he was more concerned about me than his broken Wii equipment.

'I'll be fine. Sorry about your remote, Jamie. We'll get a new one, OK?'

'She's so weird, Mum. One minute she's fine and the next she's all …' He made circles against his temples with his forefinger, whistling loudly. 'Talk about Jekyll and Hyde.'

Here, Jamie had hit on one of my private suspicions. Phoebe's tendency for extreme randomness was one of the things I wanted to talk to Desmond about. After vacuuming up the mess, I settled an unrepentant Phoebe in front of a DVD and grabbed two stools from the breakfast bar, positioning them near the threshold of the kitchen so that I could watch her movements carefully but still talk without being overheard.

'So, how's the head?'

Gently, I rubbed two fingers over the sore spot. 'I'll live,' I said, grimacing. I could feel a bump forming and knew what a sight I must look, with my unruly hair raked back behind my ears, but I was so at ease in Des's presence that I really wasn't too bothered.

'That was a bit left field, wasn't it? Has she done that before?'

I shook my head then winced as the pain rebounded around my eardrum. Pincering the top of my nose to try and staunch a looming headache, I said, 'Well, she's only chucked china thus far so I guess she's decided to branch out.'

Des raised his eyebrows, a smirk on his face. 'Greek, is she?'

I slapped his knee. 'Stop it,' I chuckled, rising to make us both a cup of tea. After switching on the kettle I turned to face him, leaning back against the worktop. 'The thing is, these incidents come so out of the blue. There doesn't seem to be an identifiable trigger – she's engrossed in something then suddenly she grabs the nearest object and strikes. It's like *Star Wars* around here.'

We both laughed but I quickly grew serious. 'It does worry me, though, Des. It's like there's two different girls in there. One of them is lovely but … well,' I lifted my hand and tilted it from side to side, 'when I say lovely, I mean nowhere near as bad as the other one …' I paused as I handed him his drink, gathering my thoughts. 'Do you think it's possible that she *is* two different people?' I asked, taking Jamie's earlier comment at face value. It was a theory I had mulled over as I had lain awake the previous night and now I voiced my fears they seemed ever more likely.

'As in multiple personality disorder, you mean?'

I nodded. 'You read my report – the pen incident, the smearing?'

'Yes, disturbing to see in a wee young thing.' His brow furrowed. 'But what makes you think …?'

I described how Phoebe moved rapidly from lucidity to vagueness, with no apparent pattern. He listened with interest, his right hand stroking emerging stubble on his chin. 'It's as if every now and then a little alarm goes off in her head signalling her to embark on some nutty escapade. When calm Phoebe returns, I try to talk to her about it but she's completely blank, as if she can't even remember behaving so bizarrely.'

Des let out a long breath. 'Who knows what we're dealing with here but I very much doubt it has anything to do with multiple personalities, although it does no harm to consider all possibilities. Any input from CAMHS?'

I huffed. 'Phoebe's social worker doesn't seem to think that's necessary.'

'There just doesnae seem to be enough money in the pot to go round these days.' Des sighed, and frowning, he stared into his cup as if closely examining his tea. 'It's lucky she came straight to you, you know. I know it probably doesnae feel like it at the moment but I suspect you're already making in-roads with her if your past record is anything to go by. I cannae help but think she'd have been a child who got passed around all the carers in the area before finding one experienced enough to help her.'

We fell silent for a moment. Shamed, I remembered how near I had come to moving her on, only that morning. When I looked up again Des was watching me keenly.

'You wasnae going to carry on with her yourself this morning, was you?'

'How did you know?'

'I could tell by your voice,' he said softly. 'I know you better than you know yourself, Rosie Lewis.'

Becoming aware of the first prickles of a flush, I rose briskly and rifled through the contents of the fridge. I could feel his eyes on my back, reminding me of the time, a couple of years earlier, when Des had made a casual invitation to take me out to dinner. Wary of the impact it might have on Emily and Jamie I refused the offer immediately, sealing any longing I had for companionship out of reach, like the medicines in my cabinet with the childproof locks. There were times when I felt a faint twinge of regret, but at least our friendship wasn't affected. Des accepted the rejection with characteristic good humour, never mentioning it again. Anyway, he soon met someone else.

While I cooked, Des spent some time with the children. I could hear him building up to full-theatrical mode and by the time I'd peeled the potatoes he seemed to have taken on the identity of an elderly Russian. 'Zu two children simply don't understand how difficult it is for me,' he whined. 'All day I spend trekking through ze snow and still I have to cook my own dinner ven I get home. Zu only have to ask my vife. Isn't zat right, Maria?'

Jamie and Phoebe could hardly breathe for laughing.

'But, husband,' I called out from the kitchen in an embarrassingly poor Russian accent, 'tonight ve have ze rabbit you caught. I cook it for you, if you vould like?'

Des laughed and rose to leave. 'No thanks, I'd best get home. It was lovely to meet you, Phoebe. Disappointing, as ever, Jamie.'

Jamie pulled a face and planted a fake punch in Des's stomach, laughing.

Out in the hallway Des leaned in to whisper close to my ear, 'I have every faith in you, Rosie, my love. If anyone can help that young girl, it's going to be you.' He sounded upbeat but I could see the concern in his eyes as he squeezed my arm. 'Call me if you need me,' he said. 'I'll leave my mobile on at night, just in case.'

I was strangely reassured to know that he would be contactable, even though I knew there was no way I would disturb him out of hours, particularly as he and his partner had just moved in together. Yawning, I closed the door and leaned back against it, cradling my head in my hands. I stayed there for a few moments, reluctant to return to the living room and play out what was left of the day with Phoebe. If it were possible at that moment I would have erected a tent on the front lawn and retreated in there with Emily and Jamie. There were times when fostering had that effect on me, when I felt like a stranger in my own home.

But after seeing that Jamie could get on with Phoebe, I'd at least been able to make the decision to follow the placement through to its natural conclusion. If my own children were fine with her being there then I certainly wasn't going to give up on her. Phoebe hadn't asked to come into care and it wasn't her fault that she was autistic either. She was a young girl who needed support and I was supposed to be the adult in the relationship. Forcing myself away from the door, I planted a smile on my face and walked back into the lions' den. Habitually, I summoned a cheerful tone, clapped my hands together and said, 'Right, let's find ourselves a game to play.' The last thing I wanted was for any child to feel like they were an unwelcome inconvenience in my house.

As the four of us set up Monopoly, my temple was still throbbing from Phoebe's earlier assault and I couldn't wait for bedtime to arrive. Every throw of the dice was punctuated with high-pitched screeches and manic jerks. My patience was sustained only by thoughts of a hot, soothing bath filled with lavender oil and the mini chocolate cheesecake hidden away at the back of the fridge.

Chapter 9

Being at home with Phoebe had me in a constant state of the jitters. All my senses were on high alert, ready to absorb the sudden high-pitched screams or defend myself against unannounced air-borne crockery. Besides lobbing dangerous objects, Phoebe had an unnerving habit of creeping up on me. I'd be in the kitchen washing up or bending to retrieve a tin from the food cupboard when a prickling sensation on the back of my neck signalled that I wasn't alone; I would turn to find Phoebe standing there, watching me.

I decided it might be easier being out. Our trip to the park the previous day had passed by peacefully enough, barring a few stares and pavement dodgers, so I rose early and packed a picnic. It was such a lovely bright spring day that it felt wrong not to make the most of it and besides, I figured the time would pass a lot quicker if we were out keeping ourselves busy. As an added bonus, Emily had decided to take a break from revision for her mocks and join the rest of us, so it was with a feeling of optimism that we set off towards Dunham Massey, a Georgian house run by the National Trust.

It was a long drive but Phoebe was surprisingly calm throughout the journey, and so by the time we pulled into the stunning entrance to the grounds we were all relaxed and eager to explore the magnificent deer park before making a tour of the old house. In the idyllic setting Phoebe seemed to blossom, skipping and laughing as we ventured through a large wooded area and down to the lake. It was at times such as this when fostering felt like a genuinely rewarding, enjoyable experience. Besides the satisfaction that comes with building happy memories for a child under stress, I was able to enjoy visiting new places alongside them. Halfway through the morning a group of us gathered by Dunham's Mill for an Easter egg hunt organised by the staff. Phoebe was beside herself with excitement and yet there was no arm flapping or strange limps as she walked over to collect her clues. From the confines of my mind a voice was whispering to me, trying to tell me something about the randomness of her behaviour, but for some reason I couldn't quite turn the volume up enough to grasp what it was. Phoebe sat with Emily and Jamie, sucking on the end of her pencil with a look of utter concentration on her face, only distracted briefly by one of the stewards, whom she labelled a 'fat bitch'. She scribbled away intermittently, and I was surprised to find that, although her writing was sprawled untidily across the page, it was definitely legible.

By lunchtime we were all ravenous, so I decided to treat us to some warm chips to go with our picnic sandwiches. The restaurant was located inside a converted stable with cosy seating areas built into each block, where horses had once slept. Large oak beams were a reminder of the building's previous life, as well as the wrought-iron feeding troughs still fixed to the wall, now filled with geraniums and trailing ivy.

Jamie grabbed a tray and scanned the menu that was written on blackboards behind the counter. 'Do you serve chips on their own?' I asked the young girl by the till, closing my eyes and releasing a groan as Phoebe began retching behind me.

Emily and I exchanged glances. 'It's alright, Mum, I'll take her outside and try to find a spare table.'

By the time I left the restaurant, with a tray with four bowls of chips balanced on my outstretched arms, Phoebe had worked herself up into a frenzy. 'I WANT PORRIDGE!' she screamed, stamping her feet. 'Not chips or sandwiches or any disgusting stuff, just PORRIDGE!'

'You can have porridge when we get home,' I said soothingly, disguising my horror for Jamie and Emily's benefit. I didn't want to draw any more attention than we already had and the pair of them looked mortified. 'For now, just try to nibble some chips, or even just a piece of bread.'

Two women planted their bags on a table a few feet away from the one Emily had claimed and gave us a cool inspection. They were well-dressed in trendy clothes, each with a patterned scarf arranged in evenly sized loops around her neck. I was accustomed to cupped whispers and double takes when I was with foster children, whether it was because of their bad behaviour, outlandish names or unusual physical appearance, but most people made a half-hearted effort to disguise their stares. But not this pair, with their flared nostrils and narrowed lips: they were looking at us as if we smelled bad.

I remembered the looks I got when I took three-year-old Alfie out. With patterns shaved into his number one crew cut, the centre of each eyebrow removed and a silver stud in one ear, we never failed to gain negative attention.

'No, blwah.' Phoebe doubled herself over, making a show of retching loudly. Although she had genuinely gagged in the past, I was beginning to suspect this current drama was an act.

There was a tensing in the posture of the two women as they each lowered an immaculate-looking toddler into a high chair, an indiscreet exchange of glances. I tried my best to ignore them, ushering the children to sit around our table. The two women drew out their own chairs and sat down, making sure they positioned themselves to get a good view. Their open-mouthed, unblinking expressions unnerved me but the more they stared, the less I felt like moving. I wasn't going to be cowed into abandoning our table just to suit them. They continued to size us up as I finally managed to persuade Phoebe to take a seat next to me.

As if their smug superiority needed any more fuelling, Phoebe suddenly raised the stakes, angrily sweeping our bowls of chips from the table, then throwing her head back, screeching with alarming force.

One of the women winced at the sound, as if her eardrums had been physically twanged. Then, leaning in, the pair huddled together and spoke in loud whispers. A light wind masked their voices so I only caught the tail end of the sentence. '... people really need parenting classes ... allowed to breed like that,' said one. Her friend nodded in wholehearted agreement, shooting me a sharp look.

I drew a deliberately long breath, wanting to correct them but resisting the urge. My own pride shouldn't come into it, I told myself. Phoebe had as much right to be there as they did, I thought, surprising myself with the strength of protectiveness I felt towards her. 'I'm sorry for the noise,' I called across to them, although it was clear that they weren't interested in pleasantries from 'someone like me'. What I really wanted to say was that they were in danger of indigestion with all the air they were sucking in through their gaping mouths.

'That's quite alright,' one woman said airily, with the patronising air of an accomplished mother confronted with apparent Slummy Mummy. In spite of the politeness in her tone, I knew there was no genuine warmth there. I could have told them then that I wasn't Phoebe's mother, but suddenly I had no urge to do so. It was perverse, I suppose, but withholding information from them gave me a sense of satisfaction – I didn't care, let them judge me.

In that moment I could understand why people sometimes behaved in outlandish ways as a form of protest, perhaps by having offensive tattoos or pierced body parts. It was a strangely pleasurable power, being able to irritate the snooty women simply by being there.

Later in the afternoon, as we were queuing for an ice cream, we encountered the same two women: they joined the queue just behind us, their toddlers standing patiently by their sides, still looking remarkably spotless.

'Can I just have some chocolate, Rosie?' Phoebe asked. 'I don't like ice cream, blwah, yuck!'

There was a quizzical cast to their eyes as they ran over our hotchpotch group, finally settling on Phoebe. One of the women opened her mouth to say something but perhaps she noticed a reserve in my stance because she faltered and closed it again.

'Yes, OK, honey,' I said, still aware of the woman's internal battle. She was probably unsure as to whether to risk having a conversation with a mother so disgraceful as me. A moment later and curiosity had evidently got the better of her.

'So, do your children not call you "Mummy" then?' she asked, her face contorting like she was chewing a wasp; she couldn't disguise her disapproval.

'I'm a foster carer so, no, she doesn't call me Mum.'

As soon as I uttered the word 'foster' they both noticeably thawed. One of them clapped her hands to her face: 'Oh, I could never do that! Could you, Celia?'

I cringed, wondering how on earth Phoebe must feel being spoken about as if she was a hot potato that no one wanted to be left holding.

'Oh no, I just couldn't!' Celia cried. 'I'd get too attached.'

Somehow I doubted that to be true. The pair of them hunkered round to include me and suddenly I was part of a triangle. Shifting uneasily, I turned back to the children, trying not to notice that I was being rewarded me with benevolent, apologetic smiles.

Chapter 10

Over the next couple of days Phoebe's behaviour began to improve and her symptoms seemed to lessen. Not to the point where she could be regarded as an ordinary eight-year-old girl, far from it, but as the Easter holidays drew to a close, and Phoebe had been living with us for almost two weeks, I noticed a definite reduction in her parroting and arm flapping.

I also became aware of a growing warmth between the two of us. It was strange, but the disapproving 'shiny' mums from our day out had stirred the instinct of a lioness within me and I felt an increasing protectiveness towards Phoebe. The experience had definitely brought us closer and she began to 'accidentally' brush against me as she passed by. It was more of an aggressive lunge than a hug, but still, I felt the right sentiment was there. Perhaps she sensed my growing fondness and was merely responding to that.

Jamie was also spending more time with Phoebe, something I hadn't bargained on. She followed him around like a loyal puppy in awe of its owner, but rather than being irritated by it, as I would have expected Jamie to be, he tolerated the attention with good humour. An easy intimacy crept into their play and I began to suspect that he actually enjoyed having someone look up to him. I knew he welcomed the privileges that came with no longer being the youngest, like not being the first to bed, for instance.

There was also more coherence to Phoebe's conversation, less 'off the wall' rambling. I couldn't help but wonder if it was Emily and Jamie's influence that had helped her to 'normalise' her behaviour.

So it was that once more I felt hopeful that we were over the worst and Phoebe wouldn't feel unhappy enough to need to soil herself again. But at 8.30am on the first Monday after the holidays, as I stood next to her in the playground of Englebrook House School, I felt an unpleasant ache rising in my throat. Watching the other children play, I couldn't help but feel that Phoebe didn't belong there. Her body language told me that she felt exactly the same way.

Despite being away from her friends for two weeks, she showed no interest in seeing any of them, and they certainly made no attempt to include her in their games. Instead Phoebe hovered at my side, her face turned into my shoulder, staring avidly at my coat. Looking around, there were several children I recognised as having Down's syndrome, a few that were wheelchair bound and others who walked with strange gaits, much as Phoebe had done when she arrived, two weeks earlier.

The playground itself was cheerful and welcoming, with lots of different play areas marked out in bright colours, and shiny mobiles hanging from the gables of various school huts. There was a fenced zone with adventure play equipment and, beyond a concrete area, a large grassed field with a running track and football nets.

'Can you see any of your classmates here yet?' I asked Phoebe. Reluctantly she pointed a number of children out to me and I gently placed my hand on her back. 'Go on then, go and say hello to them. Have a play.'

She groaned, then wandered a few feet away, before turning around to look at me. I flapped my hand at her. 'Go on,' I said, trying to encourage her to join in. 'Off you go.'

She rolled her eyes and shuffled along, turning in one direction and then the other. She seemed to fix her gaze on someone, then head towards them only to change her mind at the last minute and do an about turn. After a few minutes she began circuiting the playground, trudging unhappily along with her head lowered. Weirdly, her strange gait had returned. It was a heartbreaking sight and I really felt for her as I watched her loping along.

And that's when it hit me.

I sensed the realisation with full force, a jolt to my stomach so strong that I felt my chest constrict. It was a moment when everything else seemed to move in slow motion, only my thoughts sharpening as they raced around my mind. Phoebe wasn't stumbling along because she was struck intermittently by faulty wiring in her brain, a symptom of her autism, she was *choosing* to copy the children around her.

It was a feeling, I came to realise, that I had held in the deep recesses of my gut for several days, but now it had risen, embedding itself as a conviction firmly in the forefront of my mind.

When the school bell rang and the children were asked to line up outside the assembly hall my thoughts were still tumbling over themselves, but my shoulders sagged with relief. It had been difficult to watch her regress and I was glad that she would soon be out of my sight. Phoebe gave me a small wave before heading off to join the back of one of the lines. To me she looked to be on the verge of tears. There was lots of noisy, excited chatter as the classes filed in, though no one turned to talk to her.

The playground gradually emptied around me as parents headed for the school gates. I had phoned ahead and asked if I could have a brief chat with Phoebe's class teacher, largely to introduce myself but also to see if I could glean any more information about her condition.

The receptionist smiled brightly after buzzing me in through the main school entrance doors. She made a quick phone call and a few minutes later a rotund woman of around 50 or so arrived in reception, smiling warmly.

'You must be Rosie?' She held out her hand. 'I'm Miss Angel, Phoebe's class teacher. It's lovely to meet you.'

'What a wonderful name!' I smiled.

'Yes, you wouldn't believe how much it helps the children who are worried about moving classes. They think I couldn't possibly be anything other than kind to them.'

'Which you are, of course.'

She laughed, gesturing me through to a small side room off a corridor decorated with children's paintings. 'So, how's she been?' she asked once the door closed behind us. Her face was full of concern. 'We were all so shocked about what happened. We had to report what she'd told us, of course, but we never expected her to be taken so suddenly.'

'Erm, well, she's coping OK,' I said slowly, 'though we've had a few challenges so far.'

Miss Angel nodded. 'Phoebe does have complex needs. We've had a few frights along the way but her parents cope marvellously with her. They must be devastated. Such a lovely couple, they've done such a lot for Englebrook. Been very generous. It was Mr Steadman who donated the sundial in the main playground, you know.'

'How does she cope at school from day to day? Does she have any friends?'

'She's not terribly popular with her classmates, I'm afraid. She tends to hit out quite a lot and they've learnt to avoid her.' She grimaced. 'I'm afraid the staff have had their fair share of problems with her too.'

'Do you ever get the impression that she's …?' I hesitated, licking my lips. What I was about to say seemed disingenuous to imply, but if my suspicions were correct, something needed to be done to help her. 'Do you ever get the impression that she's putting her symptoms on?'

Miss Angel looked taken aback. 'No, of course not – why would she?'

Yes, why would she? I thought, as I made my way back to the car park. It was something I was to spend many hours puzzling over. Poor Phoebe, she didn't seem to have anyone who really understood her. Nowhere she truly belonged.

From the midst of my dreams that night, I became aware of a continuous, unsettling sound. Suspended in the free-falling world of half-sleep, I turned and bent the pillow over my ear in an effort to cling on to my relaxed state. All at once the muted, ghostly wails became increasingly shrill. Gasping, I propped myself up on one elbow, trying to gauge the time from the dim rays of moonlight dancing through a gap in the curtains. Frowning, I stayed motionless for a moment, listening to the innocuous tinkle of water running through the central heating system.

Moments after I had sunk my head back onto the pillow I heard a scream so piercing that I shot out from underneath the duvet, grasping for my dressing gown. Catching the rim of a glass of water on the bedside table, I knocked it over and it soaked the floor.

Disorientated, I stubbed my toes on the skirting board as I dashed along the hall, just as Emily and Jamie were emerging from their rooms in bleary-eyed confusion.

'It's alright, it's just Phoebe,' I reassured them.

Jamie rolled his eyes and groaned.

'You two go back to bed,' I said, a ripple in my stomach telling me that I was moments away from something incendiary. Sure enough, when I switched on Phoebe's light there it was: the explosive, grisly scene hitting my senses with full force.

Blood stains covered every visible surface of the room. The cuddly toys, so attentively arranged by Emily earlier in the week, lay scattered across the floor. With limbs and heads missing and blood-spattered stuffing strewn across the carpet, the room resembled the set of some macabre fairy tale.

My ears closed up and my vision tunnelled when I noticed that Phoebe's bed was empty. Fearing the worst, I was almost too terrified to search for her. Part of me was tempted to run back to my bedroom and crawl under the duvet. Feeling giddy, I swerved through the carnage then pulled up short.

My heart reared up with shock, slamming against my ribcage with such force that my vision wavered for a moment. Blinking, I saw Phoebe slumped lifelessly in the corner of the room; her face was white as fresh paper.

Chapter 11

Phoebe was withdrawn when I drove her home from hospital later that day. She sat listlessly in the back of the car, her head resting against the interior of the door. Her face was still pale, although now I realised this was probably more down to shock than anaemia. The emergency paediatrician had kindly reassured me that blood loss from the deep cut she had scored into her arm was unlikely to have been more than a few dessertspoons, despite the scene of massacre in her bedroom. She'd been lucky, though: if she'd hit on an artery it could have been a different story. I shuddered at the thought.

'You must be exhausted, honey,' I said, glancing at her reflection in the rear-view mirror. It was the first time I had actually willed her to mimic me. She didn't, hardly reacting at all. Her blue eyes stared glassily ahead. I wasn't even going to attempt to discuss what she'd done to herself, not yet. She needed time to recover physically before I drained her further, I felt. But how long to leave it? I wondered. And would she even remember doing it by the time we spoke?

I winced as I cast my mind back to the early morning, ambulance men negotiating their way through the decapitated teddies to reach the injured patient. Phoebe lay in a hysterical heap on the floor, spurred into life by the sight of strangers in her room. I watched as the paramedics knelt beside her, trying to examine her wounds, her fending them off with wild kicks and ferocious screeches. All I felt then was relief; at least she was conscious.

The police had interviewed me while Phoebe's injury was glued together by a doctor. It was only a formality and yet I couldn't help but feel responsible for the whole episode. Upon interrogation from nursing staff, Phoebe had admitted to stealing a pair of scissors from the kitchen while I was washing up. Children in foster care often become experts in subterfuge and although I never suspected that she was likely to self-harm at such a tender age, I felt I should have been more alert to the possibility.

Sneaking the scissors up to her room, she had stowed them under her pillow and slept with them there all night. That revelation in itself was shocking enough but the realisation that an eight-year-old girl was disturbed enough to gouge a hole in her arm on waking rocked me to the core.

I realised it would be difficult ever to relax with Phoebe in the house; I would have to stay continually on guard.

Once indoors I planted Phoebe in front of the television. Absorbed deep in a world of her own, she sank into a bean-bag and stared blankly at the screen.

I was about to call my mother and arrange to collect Emily and Jamie from her house when the handset vibrated in my hand: it was Lenke. I walked into the garden where we could talk in private, watching a listless Phoebe through the glass of the patio doors.

'How is she doing now?'

Hearing the social worker's reproving tone, I instantly bristled. 'She's a bit withdrawn but physically there's no long-term damage, thank goodness.'

'Hmmm. Have you reviewed your safeguarding procedures? Her parents are furious that this happened in the foster home, as you can imagine. They'll try and use this to discredit the local authority, of course.'

'It was an ordinary pair of household scissors, Lenke. If I'd had any idea at all that Phoebe was vulnerable to self-harm I would never have allowed her access to them. As it is I've had to hide the washing up liquid and soaps, all the toiletries, even toothpaste – she devours it all.'

There was a moment's hesitation. A cough. It was then that the realisation dawned on me.

'You knew,' I said slowly, feeling a prickle of heat. 'She's done this sort of thing before, hasn't she?'

'Well,' another pause, then, 'the school mentioned some risky behaviour in the reports but we've only just had time to read through them.' She offered this information in a casual tone, as if it were an amusing anecdote that might set me off chuckling. I wondered why the school hadn't mentioned anything to me, then I realised what her teacher must have meant when she referred to 'a few frights along the way'.

'You knew she was a self-harmer? Why wasn't I told?'

'Like I said, we're still sifting through the information but we need to make sure that nothing like this happens again.'

'How do you suggest I do that – handcuff her to the bed?' Admittedly it wasn't the subtlest of replies but I was in no mood for diplomacy.

'There's no need to take that attitude.'

'I'm sorry, I shouldn't have said that but I'm afraid there's no way I can guarantee her safety, Lenke. Her problems are too severe. As it is I can't take my eyes off her in the day, not for a minute. How am I supposed to keep her safe during the night – lock her in a padded room? And don't you think it's time to bring CAMHS in now? Something has to be very wrong for her to feel the need ...'

Lenke interrupted me. 'Phoebe is already under the consultant for the autism.'

I gripped a handful of hair and pulled it back from my forehead as I listened to her, pacing the patio with impatience. 'Self-injury is common in sufferers and the hospital have no concerns about her home life. I've discussed this with Mr Steadman and he said that her symptoms were bound to be more troublesome during times of change or stress. He says that is all the more reason for the foster carer to be extra vigilant.'

Sighing, I stopped mid-pace and leaned my head against the glass, shielding sunlight from my eyes to get a clear view of the living room: the beanbag was empty. With a sinking feeling, I yanked the door open in one swift motion, hurrying from room to room.

'So anyway, since we've discussed Phoebe on the phone, I'll log this call as one of my visits, yes?'

'Fine, yes,' I agreed quickly, saying a hurried goodbye before I realised what she was actually asking. Where on earth was Phoebe? Charging up the stairs, I finally found her standing stock-still in the middle of her room, a guilty grin spread across her face.

'What have you been doing up here, Phoebe?'

'*What have you been doing up here, Phoebe?*'

I sighed, not realising that in less than 10 minutes I would find out why she was looking shamefaced.

Even in the context of the last, difficult week, when I went downstairs and opened the post the kicking, smearing, mimicking, even the self-harming, paled into insignificance next to the contents of one of the letters. The envelope was hand-written and so, as I knew it was unlikely to be a bill or circular, it drew my attention immediately.

I tore it open, immediately registering the signatures at the bottom of the page: Will and Carolyn x.

It was Tess and Harry's new parents, who had recently adopted the two toddlers I had fostered. A slow nausea rose in my throat as the words, 'very sorry', 'clean break' and, 'really feel it's for the best' jumped out at me. Confused, I scanned the letter over and over again, trying to take in its contents. Slowly the message surfaced – they had come to the 'difficult' decision that it was best not to allow me to stay in touch with the children.

Will and Carolyn had been advised not to cut ties with me when they adopted the siblings since children can suffer lifelong depression if early attachments are severed. Scrutinising the letter again, I began to absorb their apologetic reasoning. It seemed Tess and Harry had spent their first few weeks searching for me – in cupboards, behind doors – unable to take in their loss. Now, five weeks later, they finally seemed to accept their circumstances and their new parents were concerned that seeing me would set them back and start their grieving process all over again.

Sinking into the sofa, I gripped the letter in my hand and held it to my chest. It was horrible to think that the children I had cherished for nearly three years had been searching for me. A wire of guilt passed through me at the thought of them feeling so abandoned. In turmoil, I tried to absorb the prospect of never seeing the siblings again.

Sensing someone near, I looked up and noticed Phoebe hovering in the doorway. She was staring at me strangely and I assumed she was confused by the look on my face. Slowly, she drifted into the room and sat beside me on the sofa, close enough for me to feel the warmth from her thin body. Was she seeking comfort after the tribulations of this morning or had she somehow intuited my despairing mood? Whatever the reason, I was touched and grateful for her gentleness. Instinctively I responded, wrapping my arm around her shoulder.

It was then that she slipped her hand into my own, tilting her face up to smile at me. The grotesqueness of her twisted features hit me first, before I registered the slippery feel of her palms against my own and the dank, acrid smell rising from my lap.

Phoebe had soiled in her own hand, catching me completely unawares.

By dinnertime my nerves were so shredded that when Phoebe made a grab for Jamie's fork I felt my hackles rise. 'Put that down,' I snapped. 'You only need a spoon for porridge.'

'Fuck off!' she spat.

I raised my finger and, waggling it in front of her face, I burst out: 'Don't talk like that in this house,' oscillating emotions making my voice quiver. It wasn't the swearing that unsettled me so much as the look in her eyes. Not simple defiance, something far more disturbing: pure, unequivocal hate. 'Now, go to your room and stay there. Do you hear me?'

Her gaze remained bold and challenging but I was relieved to see that she wasn't going to put up a fight. She slipped quietly from her chair and left the room.

Chapter 12

It took some heavy-duty self-coaching that night to convince myself to stick with the placement. Phoebe had looked at me with such hatred that my instincts were screaming at me to put as much distance between her and the rest of the family as possible. Digging deep, I forced myself to draw on my drive to heal, on my past experiences, and the amazing turnarounds I'd witnessed before, so that I could turn the dislike I was feeling into empathy. She must have been hurting badly to feel so much hatred, her self-harming told me that. Once I felt more forgiving, I decided that the first thing I should do was to broach the subject of self-harm with her.

After rehearsing the conversation in my mind overnight, I invited her to sit next to me on one of the fluffy beanbags in her room once she had washed and dressed, hoping she was in one of her more coherent phases. Since she flipped from rational to illogical several times in any one hour, catching her at the right time was simply a matter of chance.

I nudged her playfully with my shoulder. She smiled, nudging me back. It was a positive start.

'How's your arm feeling this morning, honey?'

From her hesitation and the way she stared at her forearm, almost in surprise, I got the impression she was thinking, what on earth is that bandage doing there? After a moment she shrugged and reached for a shiny bracelet on her bookshelf that had grabbed her attention. 'It's OK,' she said, making a move to get up.

I decided to move the focus to a previous, fictional placement. In the past I had found that children were fascinated to hear about others in a similar position to their own, particularly when I regaled them with tales of naughty exploits. It somehow helped them to conceptualise their own situation without the associated pain.

'I looked after another little girl once. She was about your age ...'

Phoebe swung back to face me again, immediately interested. 'What was she like?'

'She was VERY badly behaved,' I said dramatically.

Delighted, Phoebe giggled. '*Was* she? What did she do?'

'She painted our cat red. When I told her off, she cut off all the buttons from her school coat and dropped them down the toilet.'

Phoebe gasped, clapping her hands over her mouth. It was funny how unaware she was of her own suspect behaviour. Totally unaware of the irony, she squealed, 'That is *very* naughty! What was her name?'

My eyes moved upwards to the creative area of my brain. 'Jessica,' I lied. There was a hesitation before I continued. 'There were reasons why she behaved in that way, though.'

'What reasons?'

Studying her face, I replied slowly, 'Sometimes she felt unhappy about things that had happened to her, but she didn't feel she could tell anyone about it. It was difficult to keep such big things to herself so she behaved badly as a way of letting all those sad feelings out.'

Instead of asking for more details, as I expected, Phoebe fell silent, turning her gaze back to the bookshelf.

'I want you to feel you can talk to me if you're feeling sad, instead of ever hurting yourself again. Will you do that, Phoebe?'

'*Will you do that, Phoebe?*'

The asinine grin had returned and, with a sinking heart, I knew our conversation was over.

My dark mood lingered through the rest of the week. Every now and again a lump rose in my throat with thoughts of Tess and Harry, knowing I would have to break the news to Emily and Jamie that we wouldn't be seeing them again. I pushed the thoughts aside – Tess and Harry were safe and well cared for, I knew that. Phoebe was the one who needed my help now and I determined to put all my energies into doing just that.

Trapped

By Friday afternoon, when I picked Phoebe and Jamie up from school, I had reached the point where even my accomplished acting skills were stretched and it was difficult to summon a cheery smile. Phoebe was back on form again after the self-harming incident four days earlier, repeating every word Jamie uttered as I ushered them both into the car. I heard him sigh as he fastened his seat belt beside me and another blade of guilt passed through my chest; he looked frazzled.

I was about to pull him into a quick bear hug when Phoebe lunged forward with a wet finger outstretched, trying to smear his face with her drool. 'No,' I yelled, twisting in my seat and catching hold of her wrist. 'I've had enough and so has Jamie! Now sit back and put your seat belt on.'

'*Sit back and put your seat belt on*.'

Jamie groaned. While counting silently backwards from 20 to one I made a mental note to teach my son the same technique.

'Sorry,' I mouthed at him, trying to bestow what I hoped was an encouraging smile.

Fortunately for him, one of his football club friends had invited him for a sleepover. When we arrived at Ben's house he leapt from the car with gusto, tearing down their path like a boy released from a burning building. I couldn't blame him; I felt like taking off somewhere myself.

'Argh, it's going to be SO boring with just you,' Phoebe whined as we pulled away, dropping back against the tan leather headrest and bumping against it several times. 'What are we going to do now?'

She knew exactly what we were doing. I had taken her through the day's itinerary several times since she'd woken at 6am, knowing that autistic children feel more at ease when they follow a precise routine.

'We're going to meet some other foster carers and play with the children they're looking after. Do you remember?'

Jenny, a woman in her 50s who began fostering just over a year ago, lived in a lovely house near the river and a group of us carers met regularly at hers, to share the frustrations of being closely involved with social services and generally offering support to one another. Whenever one of our group accepted a new placement, the others were always keen to meet them and I knew they were all intrigued by my description of Phoebe. I had called ahead to warn them I would be bringing her along, if only so that Jenny could ensure her liquid soap was out of reach.

As I crossed over a wide bridge, Phoebe leaned forward, shouting in my ear, 'If I see any babies there, I'm going to kill them. I'm going to stab them with a knife and twist it 'til they're dead!'

'What did I tell you about that, Phoebe? You mustn't say nasty things, it's upsetting.'

She spent the rest of the journey repeating 'It's upsetting, it's upsetting,' over and over again so that by the time I turned into Jenny's wide, tree-lined road I had counted backwards several times. 'Here we are,' I said, forcing joviality as I secured the brake. 'Out we get.' Phoebe leapt from the car and spun in circles, her arms flapping up and down in super-fast motion. I wondered what the girls would make of her, and the other foster kids, for that matter. It was an alarming sight, particularly with her blue eyes swivelling in unison.

Rachel, a foster carer who wouldn't look out of place in a nightclub, pulled up behind my Vauxhall. I first met her two years earlier, on a paediatric first aid course. The moment she appeared in the classroom and took the seat next to mine, I knew we would be friends. Tall and curvy, she wore sparkly eye shadow and bold red lipstick. The curious fusion of glamour and mumsiness conjured an image of a nurturing 'madame'. It was clear that she had a personality to match her bright wardrobe and soon we were bellowing with laughter.

She was dressed in her customary tight skirt and colourful, silky vest top, a cluster of bracelets jingling as she waved at us before reaching into the back seat of her car to pick up her latest charge. Katy was eight months old and had only been with Rachel for three weeks, but the little one was already attached, crying whenever she left her sight.

Phoebe rushed over and planted her face barely two centimetres from Katy's.

I followed quickly behind.

'Be nice, Phoebe,' I warned.

'I like your baby, lady …'

Rachel's brightly made-up face lit up with a wide smile. 'That's nice – I expect she likes you too. I'm Rachel, and you must be Phoebe. Rosie's told me all about you.' A whizz with young children, Rachel grinned and hunched her shoulders at Phoebe while taking a subtle step backwards to give the baby some breathing space. 'Shall we go in and you can help me give her a bottle, if you'd like?'

'I'd rather eat the baby,' Phoebe said in an earnest voice. 'Can I bite her? I have sharp teeth – we could see what colour her blood is.'

Rachel looked at me and chuckled. 'Well, that doesn't sound too healthy, if you ask me, honey. But tell you what, I have some cakes in this bag – why don't you carry it in, give it to Jenny? We can eat some of those instead.'

Phoebe shook her head. 'No, yuck, I only eat porridge or chocolate.' She turned abruptly, bounding off up the path. The door was eagerly opened by Jenny; despite being in her early 50s the foster carer gave off a youthful aura, with her slim figure and keen, intelligent face.

'Hello, lovey, so wonderful to meet you! Come in, come in! I'm Jenny. I bet your name's Phoebe, am I right?'

'*Am I right?*' Phoebe sneered, surprising Jenny by squeezing past so forcibly that the foster carer almost lost her footing.

'I'm sorry,' I mouthed as I reached the door, closely followed by Rachel and the baby.

Jenny laughed and hugged me freely. 'You did warn us,' she said under her breath, giving my shoulder an affectionate squeeze.

She led us into a large living room, with a double set of large patio doors at one end overlooking a well-maintained, child-friendly garden. A large sofa was placed either side of a long coffee table, with several armchairs dotted around the space as well. On one of the walls was a framed tapestry of a child's handprint with the words, 'Quiet down cobwebs, dust go to sleep, I'm rocking my baby and babies don't keep,' embroidered in the cloth. Her house was immaculate, with a lingering smell of furniture polish, but it was comfortable too, and Jenny was so laid-back that I wasn't terrified to sit down in case I crumpled the cushions, which was just as well, because Phoebe had already made herself at home. She was jumping up and down on one of the sofas and she still had her shoes on.

'Get down from there, Phoebe,' I said, striding forward with my arm outstretched.

'Come on, let's get you some colouring out, shall we?' Jenny chipped in.

Phoebe jumped off the sofa in an instant, skipping off to follow Jenny. Her skills at distraction were impressive and I felt grateful that a battle had been averted.

Jenny returned a few minutes later, having settled Phoebe at a wooden table on the patio, a large assortment of pens and crayons laid out in front of her. She had left the garden doors open just an inch, probably so that we could talk in private.

'Here he is!' she cried as a dark-haired little boy walked shyly into the room, a cuddly toy clutched in his hand. He made straight for Jenny, burying his face in her skirt before peering shyly at us from behind her legs.

'Hello, Billy,' I said, crouching to greet him. Rachel, with Katy in her arms, waved hello with her free hand.

Billy glanced up at Jenny several times, seeking reassurance. I could almost visualise the thoughts behind those questioning eyes. Were these adults to be trusted or were they like the ones he had known before? Three years old, Billy had been placed with Jenny five months earlier due to severe neglect. The change in him over that period was staggering. She smiled down at him.

'You remember Rosie, don't you, sweetie? And that's Rachel,' she murmured softly.

'Wosie and Wakel,' he lisped sweetly, daring a smile.

'What have you got there, Billy?' I asked. He glanced up at Jenny again. On another smile from her he walked over and rested a plump hand on my knee, lifting his cuddly toy until it was a few centimetres from my eyes.

'Bunny,' he said. 'Jenny got him for me.'

I felt a moment's tightening in my stomach, a longing for the all-encompassing, defining comfort that young children offer.

Jenny grinned, her expression doting. 'Come on, Billy. Let's introduce you to Phoebe and you can do some colouring with her.' I felt a familiar prickle of anxiety as she took Billy's hand and led him to the table, wondering whether Phoebe could be trusted to be in such close proximity with a little one. So I took a seat in one of the armchairs nearest the garden, close enough to leap up at the first sign of trouble.

While the kettle boiled, Jenny answered the door to Liz, a former primary school head teacher who had made the decision to give up the position she had worked hard to achieve so that she could focus on her ambition of improving the futures of under-privileged children by helping them achieve academically.

Jenny came in with a tray laden with tea, pastries and biscuits. As Rachel reached for her tea, I marvelled at how she found time to match her lipstick with her nail polish. Running my bitten fingernails through my own less than neat hair, I realised I could learn a few lessons from her.

'So how's it going?' Liz murmured, lowering herself onto a bright pink beanbag next to the sofa.

'Apart from the plate-throwing, kicking, swearing and self-harming, you mean?' I answered wryly. 'Couldn't be better. How about you?'

Liz had recently taken on a 14-year-old girl who had worked her way through four carers in three months. I knew she was reluctant to give up on her but it was clear her extreme behaviour was taking its toll on the family.

Liz dragged her hands down her face and sighed. 'I had to take her to A&E the other day. She came in around lunchtime, staggering around the house like she'd had a stroke. Her eyes were glazed over and she couldn't formulate her words, not that she's that coherent at the best of times. Anyway, doctors couldn't work out what was wrong with her and gave her a CAT scan. Turns out the girl had inserted a tampon inside herself – soaked in gin.'

'*What*?' we exclaimed in horrified unison. 'Why?'

Liz rolled her eyes. 'New craze, apparently. The smell is undetectable that way and they can get away with consuming litres of the stuff, even at school.'

'*No*!' We stared at each other in amazement and I made a mental note to contact Ellie, the glamorous local authority tutor, so that she could add yet another shocker to her list of outrageous facts.

I found myself relaxing into the armchair, the adult contact reviving me. I loved our regular meet-ups. There was a camaraderie among us that reminded me of being back at school, each of us understanding the unique challenges that came with fostering. The gossip and scandal helped me feel less isolated, part of a team, but most valuable of all was the mutual support and kindness. Our backgrounds were quite different: Jenny was the middle-class one and probably the only carer in our group who could still afford to foster if there was no allowance available. Her husband ran some sort of internet trading company based in London, staying in the city and travelling back home for weekends. With both of her own children at university, I got the impression that Jenny would have been lonely, if not for the company of the children she fostered.

Liz had been drawn to fostering after working at an inner-city school where the catchment area took in several housing estates. She had often sent the most deprived children home with a few treats tucked into their book bag but for years had longed to take a more direct role in helping to improve their long-term prospects. Often she would come out with depressing statistics about how children fared once they left the care system, radiating frustration as she told us that 40 per cent of the prison population had spent time in care as children and almost one third of fostered children leave school with no qualifications. Her determination to make a difference was inspiring and I loved her company, but of all the foster carers I knew Rachel was the one I probably felt closest to.

In many ways we mirrored each other in our life experiences. Soon after the birth of her second child Rachel had moved with her husband to the US, returning six months later as a single parent. During one of our coffee mornings she had tearfully confided in me that, while she had found the move to an unfamiliar country difficult, her husband had embraced all that was American, reserving most enthusiasm, it seemed, for its female citizens.

Fostering gave Rachel the opportunity to gain the large, happy family she had always yearned for, as well as helping to distract her from her own angst by turning her focus outwards. The sense of achievement she gained from helping children was gradually boosting her battered self-esteem, but, like me, Rachel was one of those carers who found it difficult to let go and so, for her, fostering was a bit of a roller-coaster ride.

'Have you heard how Tess and Harry are doing?' Jenny asked. 'Can't be long now until you meet up with them, is it?'

Jenny must have noticed my crestfallen face because she quickly added, 'Oh dear,' before I'd even managed to nod my head or gather a response. The trauma of yesterday's letter had settled into a background ache but still it was hard to ignore and there was a quaver in my voice as I spoke: 'They've decided to make a clean break – I got a letter from the couple yesterday.'

They all listened, Rachel pressing her hands to her heart and shaking her head as my eyes filled up. 'Ah, but they were so attached to you,' she said, her dangly earrings trembling in a heartfelt way as if each bead was independently attuned to our conversation.

'The inevitable happened, then?' Jenny asked.

What I needed from Jenny and the others at that moment was indignation to match my own, so I took the remark badly.

'It wasn't inevitable,' I said spikily. I wanted to dissect the new parents' failure to keep their promises of staying in touch and was ready to welcome bitter remarks from all. The more vitriol the better, as far as I was concerned. I was thirsty for it, such was the mood I was in. 'It didn't have to be that way – I could have been auntie to them and ...'

Jenny eyed me sceptically and teased: 'You would never have taken a back seat, honey, not in a million years. The poor new mummy would have been constantly fending you off.'

I possessed enough self-awareness to recognise that Jenny's remarks contained grains of truth. Probably it would have been difficult for me to stand back and not offer 'helpful' advice but that realisation made her comments prickle all the more.

'Of course she wouldn't,' I protested, a defensive edge to my tone.

Jenny scoffed. 'Yeah, right! It would have been "Are you sure *that* nursery is a good idea?" and "I really don't think they're old enough to stay with relatives while you swan off for the weekend …"'

The others joined in with a fusillade of quips, bouncing off one another with the ease that only well-meaning friends can, and I soon surrendered, laughing along with them. Despite the mockery, I could sense the flare of fellow feeling among the four of us – I knew that I wasn't alone in grieving for children lost to me. In their own way, my friends were rallying round in the best way they could – helping me to see that my fostering really shouldn't ever be about me. What mattered, over and above my own feelings, was the welfare of the children.

If we were honest, each of us drew many personal benefits from the 'job'. None of us were saints. Besides the immense satisfaction of helping someone, fostering was the perfect antidote to a sense of worthlessness. Since registering I no longer felt quite such a waste of space. And it was also true that foster carers without a sense of humour should find themselves a new career.

'They only need one mummy, honey,' Liz said as she leaned over and patted my leg.

Chapter 13

On the fourth Saturday after her arrival it was Phoebe's ninth birthday. We arrived back from the contact session with her parents armed with several large carrier bags full of presents. The hour spent with them had passed pretty much as it had the previous week. Phoebe cuddled up affectionately with her father; her mother largely ignored as she hovered beside them like a spare part, offering presents up to her daughter, who pouted sulkily and snatched them away.

Half of the gifts were still wrapped; she simply hadn't enough time to work her way through the huge pile, let alone play with any of them. Not that there were any toys, as such. The packages she had managed to open struck me as inappropriate for a young girl; there was lip gloss, jewellery, even expensive clothes, but no actual toys. Where was the Lego, colouring pens or puzzles? I wondered. From her reaction it was clear that Phoebe had little interest in any of it. As soon as we got through the door she asked Jamie if he wanted to go and play in the garden again, leaving the bags in a discarded heap at the bottom of the stairs.

It wasn't an unusual state of affairs. Most parents over-indulged their children with 'stuff' when they were in care and I often thought it was a way of easing their guilt. The trouble was, with such an abundance of possessions, the children had little chance of appreciating any of them. No item had special significance to them and not only that, but I had to try and find space to keep it all, which wasn't easy, especially when several children were in placement.

In my experience, when children were in care long-term, they learnt to expect 'easy money' with no concept of its true value. By their teenage years, those who had been in the system for years often ended up materialistically minded, with a deep-seated attitude of entitlement. It was hardly surprising that some children left care at the age of 18 believing that the world owed them a living.

Besides gifts from guilt-ridden relatives, foster carers are given a weekly allowance that must be spent on clothes and toys. From my weekly allowance I was obliged to put aside £10 in savings for Phoebe. She was also given £11.50 a week pocket money to spend on whatever she liked, far more than my own children ever got. On top of that there was a clothes allowance of £22 a week, which she was allowed to spend on items of her choice. For 11–18-year-olds the allowances were even more generous.

While children are in care, their parents' family allowance isn't stopped, even though the state pays hundreds of pounds a week to house the children elsewhere. So it was a shock for me to learn, when I first began fostering, that if a child returns home, the savings of £10 a week are paid to their parents as a lump sum, to spend as they see fit.

Fearing the lump sum would be spent on alcohol and drugs, when previous placements have come to an end I have asked for permission to pay the savings in the form of supermarket vouchers, so at least the money might be spent on food for the children, but social workers have always insisted that it is the parents' right to receive the sum as cash or cheque.

As I lugged Phoebe's heavy bags upstairs to her room, I pictured myself handing a cheque over to the Steadmans on Phoebe's return to their large detached home and bristled at the thought. It wasn't that they were clearly already wealthy, that really was none of my business, but there was something about Robin Steadman that set my teeth on edge. Perhaps it was just that he was a bit too smooth. Whatever my own feelings, it had to be said that he seemed to have developed a much closer relationship with his daughter than his wife had. It was puzzling to see how isolated Phillipa Steadman seemed whenever the family were together.

Halfway through the day I called Jamie and Phoebe in from the garden for lunch, still hardly able to absorb that they were getting on so well. Even more surprising, Phoebe was first to sit at the table and Jamie actually chose to sit next to her, clearly no longer feeling vulnerable to the threat of wet fingers or flying crockery.

Emily took a break from her revision to join us at the dinner table and I noticed that Phoebe seemed to be studying my daughter, watching her take bites of her sandwich as closely as someone who might be tested on the subject later. 'Can I try some of that?' Phoebe asked eventually as Emily picked up the next half of her sandwich.

'Of course you can,' I shot back quickly, rushing into the kitchen to prepare her a cheese sandwich, cutting it into triangles so it would appear exactly like Emily's. Racing back to the table, I planted the food straight in front of her, before she had a chance to change her mind. Emily and Jamie stared between the plate and Phoebe with their mouths open, eager to see what she planned to do with a piece of actual solid food.

Having learnt the hard way when Jamie was a toddler that being too keen for a child to eat can put them off, I drew Emily and Jamie's attention away from her, gaily prattling on about what television series we might start to watch next. We had recently caught up with all available episodes of *Lost* and had so far failed to find an equally absorbing replacement. They both fired suggestions across the table and I offered one or two of my own, all the while watching Phoebe out of the corner of my eye.

She poked the bread on her plate several times as if suspicious it might be a living organism. Apparently reassured that it wouldn't grow arms and throttle her she leaned over and took a cautious sniff. Straightening, she pinched the edge of one of the triangles between forefinger and thumb, and plucked off the tiniest piece of bread. Lifting it to her mouth, she tentatively brushed it against her lips and held it there for a long moment, as if in danger of it biting back.

For goodness' sake, just eat it, I thought, willing her to take the plunge. She did, rolling the bread over in her mouth with the relish of a child being forced to eat cotton wool. There was a pause during which I held my breath, praying she wouldn't start retching. She glanced around at us but I averted my gaze, suggesting casually to Emily and Jamie that it might be worth giving *Grey's Anatomy* a go.

Within ten minutes Phoebe had managed to eat two whole triangles, which amounted to one full slice of bread. Emily, Jamie and I exchanged furtive but exhilarated glances, both of them looking every bit as pleased as I was. It seemed such a momentous event that I was tempted to cheer but restrained myself, instead suggesting we make the most of the continuing sunshine by taking a walk to the park.

Gone was Jamie's reluctance to join in. He leapt up and asked if he could fetch the scooters from the shed so that he and Phoebe could ride there and back. If ever there was a moment when I wished I had a camera at my fingertips it was then. Phoebe's face was a picture; she looked so chuffed that my eyes actually filled up. It made me wonder whether she had ever actually had any friends of her own.

After an uneventful and therefore enjoyable trip to the park, we walked back via our local parade of shops. Phoebe stopped short outside the local charity shop, abandoning her scooter on the pavement and standing frozen to the spot, staring into the window. At first I thought she was studying her reflection and expected her to begin remonstrating at any moment, flinging her arms around manically as she had on most of our other trips.

By the time Jamie and I had caught up with her she turned to me with a pleading expression. 'Could I please buy that, Rosie? With my pocket money?'

That was a pirate's outfit displayed on a small mannequin in the window. 'Well, I'm not sure,' I said, knowing that if we bought second-hand I couldn't be sure that it was made with fire-retardant material. 'It's not new so ...' I went on, but her crestfallen expression stopped me mid-sentence. If Phoebe was my own child I wouldn't have hesitated but I knew how meticulously the rules had to be followed when caring for Looked After Children.

'Oh, please, Rosie.' She looked at me so earnestly that I thought, sod it – we were always being told to treat foster children as we would our own so I wasn't going to turn her down. How funny, I mused, as we went into the shop and the assistant retrieved the pirate dress from display – Phoebe had four bags of unopened presents in her room and yet fixated on an item that cost £2.50. As it turned out, the dress hadn't even been worn. All the labels were still attached, confirming that it was originally purchased at Marks & Spencer, which allayed my fears that it might be a rogue item from a dubious source.

Before we reached the gate Phoebe was removing her jumper in her excitement to try the dress on. Minutes later she emerged from the bathroom and performed a twirl, a huge grin plastered on her face.

'Hmm,' I said, 'looking good, but not quite the genuine article yet.'

Her face dropped. 'Why not?'

'A-ha, come with me,' I said, putting on the accent of a pirate. Energised by the improvement in her symptoms, I was pleased to find my playful side was emerging. I loved playing with children, whipping up their capacity for imaginary games. The last few weeks with Phoebe had been so draining that I'd almost forgotten she was still a child who needed to be stimulated.

So excited was Phoebe when we returned to the living room a few minutes later, adorned with one of my sequined scarves around her neck and a purple sash at her waist, that she couldn't keep still, although it was a general wriggle rather than the peculiar arm flapping/eye rolling routine. Jamie completed her delight by offering her one of his swords. When he suggested they build a camp in the garden I thought she might burst with the excitement of it all.

Although it was a joy to watch the pair as they erected blankets and duvets between the trellis and the horse chestnut tree, charging loudly in and out of their makeshift camp with swords aloft, I couldn't help but puzzle over yet another swift change in Phoebe's behaviour. Until now it had been impossible to interest her in any form of imaginative play and yet there she was, playing as if she'd never been any different.

As I poured myself a glass of lemonade and sat on the swing at the bottom of the garden, I was beginning to regret that the placement might soon end. The rest of the day passed quickly and without any tantrums or trying behaviour. At tea time Phoebe was thrilled when my mother made a special visit to wish her 'Many Happy Returns' and even ventured to try a few mouthfuls of her own birthday cake. She sat calmly by my side that evening when I read her a bedtime story and as I wished her good-night the trial of the last few weeks was all but forgotten.

How naive it was, I realised all too soon, to let my guard down so easily.

Chapter 14

It was with a renewed sense of enthusiasm that I woke the next morning, surprised to find that Phoebe was still quiet in her room, despite the time. She was usually the first awake and yet it was 6.45am and there was still no sign of her. I was halfway across the kitchen with a full kettle in my hand when a lurching sensation in my stomach stopped me in my tracks.

Instinct drew me back up the stairs. A memory of the recent bloody scene following her self-harming incident advanced my rising panic and I charged into the room without bothering to knock. My breathing gradually returned within safe limits as I scanned the room. There was no horrific smell or bloody sights and Phoebe lay serenely beneath her duvet, although she didn't look too well. Pale and sickly I can cope with, I thought, before an uncomfortable twist in my stomach nudged another possibility to the forefront of my mind.

'Phoebe, have you eaten something you shouldn't, honey?'

Her eyes were wide with hesitancy as she stared back at me, shaking her head.

'You won't be in trouble,' I said, crouching beside her bed in an unconscious gesture of supplication. If she were to trust me enough to tell me what she'd done, she had to understand that I wasn't going to be angry with her. 'But I need to know, now. You really don't look too well.'

She began to cry. 'I've got a tummy ache,' she croaked in a sickly voice.

Manoeuvring my way through the piles of half-opened presents still spread across the floor, I threw open the curtains and knelt back beside her bed, crouching to get a better look at her. 'You must tell me what you've eaten,' I said calmly, sunlight highlighting the paleness of her skin.

With effort she propped herself up on one elbow, wincing and clamping a hand to her stomach. She looked about ready to throw up but I didn't want to encourage that until I found out what it was that lay in her stomach. If it was a harsh substance it might burn her throat on the way back up. 'Phoebe, tell me,' I demanded, furious that she'd tried to hurt herself again.

She opened her mouth to speak but closed it again. There was a long hesitation before she finally lifted her free hand and pointed under the bed. Down on all fours, I lowered my head to the carpet and gasped. The space between the floor and the slats of her bed was littered with all sorts of containers. Craning my neck, I stuck my arm in as far as it would go and in a long fanning motion I swept them out so they were spread out on the floor in front of me.

Colour burned my cheeks as I took in the sight. There must have been almost 20 bottles of various shapes and sizes there, some full, others almost empty. 'Which one was it?' I asked, no longer able to disguise the urgency in my tone. 'Tell me!'

Leaning over, she pointed to a half-empty bottle of shampoo.

I snatched it up. 'This one?'

She nodded as tears rolled down her cheeks.

'How much did you drink?'

Her eyes widened but she didn't answer, instead throwing back the duvet and rushing to the toilet. She threw up almost constantly for 10 minutes solid, while I perched on the edge of the bath, rubbing her back and offering her sips of water. Every now and then she rested her head on the toilet seat in exhaustion and the anger I had felt towards her transferred to myself.

How could I have let the peace of the last day or so lull me into a false sense of security? And how on earth did she get hold of such a stash of products when I'd locked everything away from her? Then, with a fresh wave of anger at myself, I realised that she must have searched through the bags of presents from her parents and taken them from there. How stupid of me not to check through the contents before leaving them in her room.

Guilt and anxiety rivalled for my attention as I plucked a few sheets of tissue from the roll and offered them to a trembling Phoebe.

The staff at our GP surgery had always wholeheartedly supported me in my role as a foster carer and that day was no different. As soon as I explained what had happened they told me to bring Phoebe straightaway to the surgery, promising to squeeze her into their already-full schedule of patients.

After dropping Emily and Jamie at school I wrapped Phoebe in a warm coat and walked her around the corner to the surgery, supporting her as she shuffled along the pavement. It occurred to me that anyone behind us might have mistaken me for the carer of a frail old lady, the way her feet were dragging so lethargically. Inside the surgery I thanked the receptionist, who smiled kindly, before dropping her jaw in astonishment. 'No, don't do that, dear,' she said, alarmed. Whipping around, I saw that Phoebe had ducked her head under the antibacterial alcohol gel that was fixed to the wall, licking at the dispensing spout with outstretched tongue.

'Phoebe,' I groaned. How could she possibly contemplate adding to the concoction already swirling in her stomach? I anguished as I pulled her away.

'I need it,' she said as I pulled her away to the waiting room. She spoke with desperation, her tone salvaging something in my mind that I had stored away without fully considering. Lenke was wrong when she said that Phoebe ate things that weren't food; she hadn't eaten anything inedible since she came to me. She had only drank, I realised, with a rush of blood to my ears. My mind stuttered as I tried to follow what the pitching sensation in my stomach was prompting. Phoebe had ingested soap, shampoo, shower gel and now liquid alcohol gel.

I'd been so busy thinking about the signs and symptoms of autism that perhaps I'd missed what was staring me in the face. Did she feel dirty? I wondered, watching as she sank heavily into one of the hard-backed chairs and pulled her legs up towards her stomach. Could it be that the poor child was trying to cleanse herself from the inside out?

Any further revelations were forestalled by the appearance of her name on a flashing screen above our heads.

Doctor Kenwick was old school and thorough, hence his surgery always ran at least an hour behind his other, younger colleagues', so I was grateful that the receptionist had decided to allow us to jump the queue. 'What can I do for you today, young lady?' the doctor asked, peering over the top of his spectacles. He was so overweight that his stomach protruded over his belt and the buttons of his shirt appeared dangerously close to popping open, but the cheeriness of his expression more than made up for it, his deep jowls moving independently of each other as he smiled at his new patient.

'*What can I do for you today, young lady*?' Phoebe repeated, causing his smile to rapidly vanish.

'I'm sorry, doctor,' I said, marvelling that in spite of her delicate condition, she was still capable of mimicking strangers. 'Phoebe drank some shampoo during the night and now she has a bad tummy ache,' I said, producing the bottle from my bag. 'She's been sick several times this morning. We're not sure what time you drank it, are we?' I looked at her but she was in that other world of hers, flapping and rolling her eyes. 'Autism,' I said under my breath, raising my eyebrows and inclining my head towards her. I couldn't help but register the look of disgust Phoebe gave me when I said it.

'A-hh,' he nodded. 'I don't have Phoebe's notes with me as we just have her down as a temporary patient at the moment. Any idea how long she'll be with you? If it's going to be longer than 12 weeks I'll request her full notes from the previous GP. Might be helpful to have the full picture in front of us.'

Pursing my lips, I was about to reply when Phoebe suddenly ceased all movement, butting in. 'Not long. I hate it here – her house is tiny. I'm going home next week.'

'I see.' He gave me an amused wink before surveying her. 'Right, young lady, let's see what trouble you've got yourself into.'

Mercifully she sat in silence while he looked down her throat, checked her ears and listened to her chest.

'Well, nothing too much to worry about there. Let's get you on the couch and have a feel of your tummy.'

As soon as those words left his lips Phoebe began arm flapping again. '*Let's get you on the couch and have a feel of your tummy*,' she said with a nasty sneer, and then, 'No, young lady, let's not get on the couch and have a feel of your tummy. No, no!' she snapped, before falling into a round of barks so deep that the doctor pushed his glasses further up his nose and leaned back in his chair, his lined face frowning.

'Now, now, none of that,' he said eventually, standing briskly and gesturing to his examining table. 'Over you come.'

Following his lead, I rose and made to move towards him as he leaned over and pulled a protective sheet of blue tissue from a wide roll fixed to the wall, covering the white leather couch with it.

'I'll come with you, Phoebe. There's nothing to worry about – the doctor won't hurt you.'

'No, no, no,' she cried, weeping and clinging tightly to the arms of her chair. 'Please, Rosie,' she implored. 'Please, I don't want to.'

'OK, it's alright.' Returning to my seat, I reached out and took hold of one of her hands. It was damp with sweat and her legs were trembling visibly.

'Sorry, doctor, do you think you could check her over if she stands up next to me?'

Holding up his hands in surrender, he returned to his chair.

'Alright. No need to work yourself up, my dear.'

After a brief examination of her tummy, Doctor Kenwick confirmed that there was probably no long-term damage and recommended that Phoebe eat natural yoghurt for the rest of the day. It might have been the look on Phoebe's face as she clung to my arm, or perhaps sheer gut instinct, but as we left the surgery and headed for the mini-store, I became convinced that our visit to the GP had signalled a turning point in our relationship.

Sure enough, Phoebe was unusually affectionate that night as I sat beside her and read *The Little White Horse*, leaning deliberately close to me. When I reached the end of the second chapter and announced it was time for bed she looked up, staring at me in a way that made me feel as if she was sizing me up.

'Why didn't you let that man examine me?' she asked eventually.

'The doctor, you mean?'

She nodded and lowered her head as if in shyness, a trait I hadn't seen in her before. Defiance, yes, stubbornness, certainly, but never reserve. Puzzled, I stared at the top of her head, her hair now a shining and silky golden brown, having been washed and brushed through so many times since her arrival.

'Well, you were upset,' I said gently, 'and I wouldn't let anyone do anything to you that you didn't feel comfortable with, would I?'

It was a statement rather than a question but she raised her head and shook it, watching me with that same scrutinising expression. Smiling, I held out my hands with the offer of a hug. Edging her bottom closer, she laid her head against my chest, giving me rarely granted access into her personal space. Wrapping both arms around her, I drew her into an embrace and puzzled over her reaction. It was almost as if she had only just realised that she could trust me to protect her. She nuzzled her head into the space between my neck and shoulder, rubbing her cheek against my cardigan.

Minutes later, as I stood at the door and watched her climb into bed, I was once again filled with an ominous sense of dread, hoping to goodness that the thoughts darting around in my head were completely and utterly off-target.

Chapter 15

I had to collect Phoebe from school early the next day, as she had an appointment at the hospital for an initial health assessment. All Looked After Children were checked over by a paediatrician within 28 days of coming into care and I was quite looking forward to going to the hospital, eager for the opportunity to gather more information on Phoebe's history and original diagnoses.

As it turned out, my efforts the previous evening in compiling a long list of questions about her condition were a complete waste of time. The doctor's remit was to assess Phoebe's physical health and make sure she was not disadvantaged or suffering in any way due to her stay in foster care. Her emotional health was touched upon but when I tried to direct the focus towards Phoebe's autism, the paediatrician, a smart Asian man with impeccable English, swiftly returned to the structured form he had to complete.

When we reached the section covering eating habits I explained that her staple diet was porridge and the doctor, concerned that her height and weight were way below normal levels on the centile chart, recommended Phoebe be referred to a dietician. It was a step in the right direction and might be of use but I left the hospital feeling a little deflated. I wasn't sure why but I couldn't shake off the feeling that so much more could be done to help Phoebe. Clearly she wasn't going to be stretched at school; all her teachers were concerned with was getting her to reach the standard levels of literacy and numeracy expected of all their pupils. Since it was a special school with high levels of learning disabilities, this was hardly an aspirational target. I couldn't help but feel she deserved more.

We got home early afternoon, before Emily and Jamie. Pleased, I think, to have me to herself, Phoebe invited me to sit with her on the swing at the bottom of the garden. Ignoring the pile of dishes in the sink, I followed her down our weathered sandstone path to the garden swing. The overhead canopy offered partial shade for our faces, the rest of us bathed in the warm sunlight. It was a peaceful spot and Phoebe seemed to absorb the tranquillity, sinking into her seat and resting her head back on the cushions.

'Did you have a nice morning at school?'

She shook her head. 'It was boring.'

'What did you do?'

'Walked around …'

I knew she hadn't spent her entire morning circling the playground on her own, but from what I'd seen when I visited recently, there was likely to be some truth in what she said.

'What else, apart from walking around? Did you read to the teacher?'

She sat swinging her legs and saying nothing.

And after a while: 'Why didn't you let the doctor check my tummy?' There was a watchfulness in her stance, a gauging of my reaction, but she had changed the direction of our conversation so abruptly that at first I was confused.

'He didn't ask to check your tummy.'

'Not this morning,' she said, with a sigh that suggested I was being particularly slow. 'Yesterday.' She lowered her eyes to her lap. 'After I ate the shampoo.'

Her question, so out of the blue, jolted me. I couldn't help but feel once again that our visit to the surgery held a special significance for Phoebe, though I wasn't sure exactly why.

'I told you before, I would never let anyone do anything to you if you felt uncomfortable about it.'

She nodded, smiling as if my answer had satisfied her, confirming her own interpretation of events. I mulled over my options: either I could leave things as they were and let her steer the conversation any way she liked, or I could prompt her with some questions of my own. If she had nothing to say, well, no harm could come of it.

Aware that directing her would be irresponsible from a professional point of view and wary of putting ideas into her head, I revived the fictional Jessica again, knowing that, if nothing else, she would grab Phoebe's attention.

'Jessica was scared to talk to me at first. I think she felt bad about upsetting anyone, but after a while she grew to trust me. In the end she knew that she could tell me anything and I would keep her safe, no matter what.'

I waited to see if Phoebe would latch on to the conversation but she began humming, swinging her legs as I gently rocked the swing and stared out across the garden. We stayed that way for several minutes, listening to the distant chirp of birdsong, the occasional drumming of wheels on tarmac as cars slowed and accelerated off again on the other side of our hedge. I found myself clenching my teeth, willing her to open up to me.

For a while I had suspected the worst. If there was something in her history that had exacerbated her condition, I longed to help her let it out. Several times she turned to stare at me but as soon as I met her gaze she looked away. A few more moments passed before she spoke in a timid voice.

'I think I'm like Jessica,' she said, regarding me with wariness.

Resisting the urge to launch into a barrage of questions, I kept my tone casual.

'Do you? Why?'

There was a long pause, another few swings of her legs.

'I'm not allowed to tell.'

It was a time-old giveaway and I couldn't avoid the involuntary tensing that gripped my upper body. Phoebe noticed, immediately clamming up. After several moments of silence, during which time I cursed myself for not being able to conceal my reaction, I spoke in a soft voice.

'Can you tell me why you're not allowed to tell?'

She didn't speak.

Knowing it would be wrong to demand to know who had asked for her silence, I decided to try a different, gentler tack.

'Jessica was told not to tell as well, but the secret grew inside her until she felt unwell in her head. When she told me what had made her feel so bad she began to feel better.'

There was still no response. Phoebe sat unmoving beside me; even her legs had stopped swinging.

'No one can hurt you now, Phoebe. Whatever you tell me, I will keep you safe.'

In an instant she buried her face in my T-shirt and kept it there. A long silence followed while I gently stroked her hair. Her face turned to the side but I could still feel her warm breath as she rested on my tummy.

'I get scared when the noise comes,' she said eventually. 'And when his face looks like a tomato.'

'Whose face?' I asked, glad she couldn't see my own face had fired up, the heat stinging my cheeks. 'What noise?'

She sat up abruptly, screwing her features into a nasty sneer.

'*Whose face? What noise?*'

It was then that I had a sense, not yet wholly clear, that her bizarre habits were not merely imitations of the children she went to school with. More complicated than that – I suspected smoke and mirrors, a distraction invented as a way of leading everyone off the trail she was too frightened to explore.

'How does his face look like a tomato?' I tried again, knowing, before she had even repeated me again, that I had already lost her.

We sat in silence until the sky clouded over and the sunlight faded to a pale orange glow. When we went back indoors Phoebe asked to watch television, unaware of the turmoil she had provoked in my mind. Only the remains of a bright red rash that stretched from her cheeks, down her throat and to her chest gave a clue to the lingering emotion of our conversation.

'I hate you,' she spat as I switched on her favourite channel. 'I want to go back to Mummy and Daddy!'

The spitefulness, I realised, was her way of punishing me for taking her close to revealing something she sensed would be dangerous. She spent the rest of the day in a contrary mood, defensive, which I guessed might be her way of concealing the heartache I had stirred up.

It was as I was setting the table for dinner and called her to wash her hands that the festering emotion finally erupted. Phoebe stormed into the kitchen, raging with a destructive energy. With her eyes glazed over, she ripped open the doors of the cabinets and swept packets and tins from inside, hurling them at the walls and across the floor. A bottle of ketchup was pulled violently from a shelf and launched towards me as I hovered in the doorway. The onslaught was so sudden that I barely had time to react and so I stayed where I was, watching her helplessly.

There was no point in trying to stop her, I decided. Apart from the danger of being caught by flying missiles, there was an inner desolation that needed to be expressed. If she was on the rampage through temper alone then I would have stepped in and restrained her, but instinct told me that this was something quite different – an animal need to release the awful tension inside her. No, the best thing, I thought, was to wait for the anger to abate. If I'm honest, I felt more comfortable watching her express her fury that way, rather than the flapping arms and rolling eyes. This was the sort of behaviour I recognised, an angry rage at the unfairness of the world. To me, this was all familiar stuff.

When the cupboards were all but bare she stood and stamped on the heap of assorted packets and jars, screaming with a tormented rage. Spent, she collapsed onto the kitchen floor and drew up her knees, crying heavily into her hands. Sidestepping the devastation, I crouched down and stretched my arms around her, noticing how badly her body was shaking as she sobbed.

Chapter 16

That night I dreamt Phoebe was standing above me, the pair of scissors that she had used to puncture her arm held aloft and ready to strike at my heart. It was so vivid that when I woke my hair was damp with perspiration and the muscles in my legs ached with the after effects of adrenaline that had coursed through them during the night.

Instead of my usual coffee I warmed some milk, hoping to calm my agitated state of mind. The temporary soothing effect of the warm liquid was short-lived, though. A yell of distress from upstairs jerked me back to my recent state of alertness, more so because I realised it was not the usual screech from Phoebe but, alarmingly, a cry from Jamie. Knowing how much it took to rattle my son, a stark vision from last night's dreams exploded to the forefront of my mind, Phoebe's bloodied knife taunting me as I tore upstairs and into his room.

Jamie sat with his back against his headboard, clutching his duvet up to his nose and peering over the top, his eyes wide in horror. Looking every bit like an old fishwife, Phoebe stood over him with her legs splayed, one hand resting on her hip and the other waggling a pointed finger a couple of inches from his face.

'You are a dirty whore,' she growled in a voice so deep I couldn't believe it actually came from her. 'An ungrateful dirty bitch, that's what you are.'

'Get her out of here, Mum!' Jamie beseeched, appealing to me with his eyes.

Phoebe seemed to be in some kind of trance. She didn't even turn around when I called her, demanding she leave Jamie's room.

'Come on.' I slipped my hand through the arm she rested on her hip. 'You're not supposed to be in here.'

The incident gave me another flash of insight into her home life, telling me that all was definitely not what it seemed in the Steadman household.

When Jamie came down to breakfast Phoebe, oblivious to his expression, patted her chair, inviting him to sit next to her.

'No, thanks,' he said, giving her a you've-got-to-be-kidding-me look.

She appeared injured. Either she had completely forgotten the 'fishwife' incident or simply hadn't been aware of it happening in the first place. I felt sorry for her; it seemed that Jamie and Emily were the only children in her life who were prepared to pass the time of day with her, but I wasn't going to say anything to Jamie. He had every right to be annoyed with her. No schoolboy wanted to wake to the sight of Phoebe's eyes rolling and being called a 'dirty whore' into the bargain.

Breakfast was over with quickly. Although Phoebe had taken to nibbling on a few bits of 'tame' solid foods, she still wasn't eating much. Jamie vacuumed his toast up even faster than usual – eager, I think, to escape Phoebe's company. Without being asked, he cleared his bowl and plate, even dropping them into the soapy water himself rather than perching them on the side, as was his usual habit.

'Wow, thanks, Jamie!'

Pulling on a pair of yellow rubber gloves, I plunged my hands into the sink then groaned inwardly. Phoebe had left the table and followed Jamie into the living room, watching him sheepishly from behind. She was chewing her lip and I got the impression she was building up to something. Scanning my brain, I tried to think of a distraction; Jamie needed to be left alone for a while.

I flicked my gloves off and was about to invite her to help me with the drying but I was too late. Already she'd approached Jamie, eyeing him shyly.

'Can we play Wii for a bit before school, Jamie?'

'Nah, don't want to, thanks.'

Phoebe's face fell. She looked genuinely wounded.

'We really haven't got that much time, Phoebe,' I chipped in. 'We have to leave in 10 minutes.'

Jamie had noticed her reaction, I could tell by the look of tenderness that crossed his face. 'Actually, it's OK, we can play a quick game if you like.' He reached for the brand new Wii remotes and handed one to Phoebe. Her eyes lit up, beaming.

His willingness to forgive her so quickly brought tears to my eyes. As he was about to leave for the bus I stopped him in the hall, straightening his tie and tucking down the collar of his blazer.

'Thanks for what you did in there, Jamie.'

'What did I do?'

'You know, with Phoebe. Thanks for being so forgiving.'

He shrugged. 'S'alright. I feel sorry for her. There must be something *very*, *very* wrong.'

Jamie's words echoed in my mind during the school run and when I got back home just after 9am I immediately called Lenke. Having been blocked every time I tried to arrange outside support for Phoebe, I decided it was time for some plain speaking. Little did I realise, as I waited for the call to connect, that I could shake the social worker by her shoulders and scream at the top of my voice, for all the good it would do.

When she picked up I gave her a summary of my conversation with Phoebe and her explosive reaction, a few hours later: 'And so there's obviously something amiss at home. There's no way she should go back there until we've had time to explore this properly. She's going to need a bit more time to build enough trust in me. I think we're nearly there but ...'

'Phoebe's father has been on the phone again this morning. He is extremely anxious to get her back and there is no evidence that she is at any risk at home.'

Agitated by her lack of support I ran my fingers through my hair and began pacing. It seemed Lenke's focus hadn't shifted in the slightest – all she wanted to do was keep Phoebe's parents sweet, whatever facts were staring her in the face. I was suddenly reminded of something Des had told me – in some local authorities, social workers are encouraged to seek counselling if they find themselves sexually attracted to a birth parent. Des explained that there have been cases where social workers have fallen under the spell of charismatic but violent, psychopathic parents. Controlling men, those capable of severe domestic violence, often, according to Des, possess an almost demonic ability to manipulate the people around them. In one case, the father involved managed to convince two successive social workers to sleep with him, leaving them incapable of objective thought.

While I knew it was unlikely that sexual attraction was the reason for Lenke's apathy, I did worry that she was blinkered by the accent and status of parents. But how could she ignore such disturbing signs? If Phoebe was in the process of building up the courage to reach out to someone, shouldn't her social worker allow her the time and space to get to that point?

When Lenke replied it was clear that the answer was a resounding no. Using a tone that was becoming familiar: polite, long-suffering, but with a touch of strained patience, she said, 'We've been through this, Rosie. The child will be going home shortly but I'll send you a checklist anyway, if you'd like. Access to CAMHS is run on a points system: if Phoebe gets enough points from the answers you give, she will be referred, but by that point she'll probably already be home.'

With a persistence that I wouldn't have been capable of in my pre-fostering years, I challenged her, refusing to be fobbed off. 'I've sent you an email with full details of what Phoebe has said. I'd like to discuss it with the fostering team manager as soon as possible, please.'

There was a pause while Lenke composed her answer. 'There really is no need for that, Rosie. Let's make a date to discuss this next week.' Her tone was more conciliatory now but still brisk, as if she had one hundred and one more important things to do than indulge me.

'I really think we should meet before then,' I insisted. 'And Phoebe urgently needs to talk to someone with professional knowledge. I'm afraid I might be a bit out of my depth here.'

Lenke sighed, but not a sympathetic noise of concern, rather the groan of a woman who would rather get her work finished and head off home. 'I'm sorry,' she said, 'I have other commitments.'

'As soon as you can then,' I conceded with exasperation.

Immediately after I ended the call I found myself puzzling over something the social worker had said: why was it only Phoebe's father who was agitated to get her back? What were her mother's feelings in all of this?

Chapter 17

Letting myself back into the house after the school run the next morning, I felt a sudden invigoration. Lifted by being alone in the house, I felt the strain of the past few weeks slowly ebbing away. However temporary, it was a wonderfully freeing sensation and I wanted to hold onto it for as long as possible.

Making myself a coffee, I considered turning my phone off for a couple of hours. There was something festering in my mind, an inkling that I wasn't piecing together an accurate picture of Phoebe's troubles. What I wanted was to sit and absorb her words from the day when we sat on the swing, to examine the message she was giving me through the silence and then the violence that followed. To make sense of it all I needed time alone, away from the usual everyday demands.

After 10 minutes, guilt-ridden and anxious, I switched the handset back on – mums don't get to turn their phones off and still feel relaxed. Instead, I slipped it onto one of the shelves of our desk and settled myself in front of the computer with a fresh cup of coffee.

Unsurprisingly, it rang within minutes. When I saw the caller ID I rolled the office chair backwards and, in anticipation of being irritated, automatically began pacing.

'Hi, Lenke.'

'Hi, Rosie. I'm sorry I couldn't talk yesterday, I was so busy.'

'That's OK.' I was just speculating on the best way to motivate her into taking action when she took the wind out of my sails.

'There has been an emergency strategy meeting. The local authority has decided to apply for an Interim Care Order, so all future contact between Phoebe and her parents will be supervised.'

'Oh, OK,' I said, relieved. At least it was a move in the right direction. As we ended the call I wondered how Phoebe would react to the changes. It should only take the local authority a day or two to secure the order and then dealings with her parents would be on a much more official footing. With all contact supervised, there would be far less flexibility in meeting times and places. Robin Steadman would not like it, not one little bit. The thought pleased me, to such an extent in fact, that I wished I could be present when the news was broken to him.

It was unlike me to be so cold. For most of my placements I had felt sympathy for the birth parents. It was usually the case that they had been dealt an unfortunate hand in life and many simply lacked the ability to overcome such challenges, their children suffering alongside them. Robin Steadman had no such excuse: as far as I could see, he had it all.

There's no proof the man has done anything wrong, I chastised myself, settling back into the swivel chair behind the desk. Besides, I had no idea what miseries he may have gone through in his life. Money didn't guarantee immunity from suffering; I only had to look at Phoebe to know that. She had been raised in a privileged home and yet she was one of the unhappiest children I had ever come across.

With a few beeps and clicks, our family computer shook itself awake and as soon as the home screen appeared I entered a number of searches into Google: 'autism', 'intermittent symptoms', 'effects of stress on autism', 'sporadic autism'. I wasn't surprised that the resulting list was long. Millions of results had been produced but my eyes fell immediately to a hyperlink about two-thirds of the way down the first page, the words 'elimination of symptoms' and 'new cure' drawing me in.

The link took me to a website: Peach, Parents for the Early Intervention for Autism in Children. Peach was a charity formed by parents who were looking for ways to overcome the problems associated with autism. Snatching up a pen, I began scribbling notes on the jotter pad in front of me. It seemed that with intensive therapies some children had made astounding progress, all but obliterating their symptoms. Although some claimed that the condition had been cured, most reported a dramatic improvement in what they considered to be a lifelong condition.

After reading the case studies, I was filled with inspiration and eager to find out more about the therapies, particularly one that the site advocated. Applied Behavioural Analysis involved breaking down any skill that the autistic child lacked into the most basic form and then working from there to help them master the ability to do it. Absent-mindedly twirling the pen in my mouth, I found myself gripping the end with my teeth in concentration. There was so much to take in and the thought of formulating an action plan excited me. Whether it was recognising emotions from facial expressions or learning to socialise, by starting at the basics and reinforcing correct responses with positive verbal praise, it seemed almost all autistic children were capable of vast improvement, some to the point where they became indistinguishable from their mainstream peers.

I was so absorbed by the possibilities that when my alarm went off at school pick-up time, I realised I hadn't even eaten lunch. Grabbing my keys, I jogged to the car, eager to put my research into practice.

Chapter 18

'Let's play a game,' I announced later that evening when Jamie had left for football training with his dad and Emily was sitting in front of the TV watching repeats of *Doctor Who*. Instead of being dogged by a sense of defeat as I had over the past few weeks, I became aware of a new feeling, a determination to rise to the challenge of helping Phoebe to reach her full potential. It was clear she possessed a surprising degree of intelligence – her reading age roughly equalled her chronological age – quite an accomplishment considering her below-par schooling, but her symptoms seemed to stand in the way of her putting it to good use. I really felt that if we could work on her social skills and abysmal levels of self-esteem, her chances of making and maintaining friendships would vastly improve.

Phoebe immediately looked interested. She joined me at the dining table where I'd laid out strips of different coloured Plasticine on a large piece of white A3 card. From my online research I had prepared a list of tasks to work through with Phoebe, all designed to increase concentration and retrain the brain into functioning normally. Her eagerness to spend time with my son told me that she craved social interaction. My intention was to combine the 'brain training' activities with some games that would encourage the development of trust between us. Once she had faith in me, I reasoned, it would help her to react normally to strangers. Step by step, I wanted to teach her appropriate responses to every possible encounter.

But first I wanted to try a different game – one that I had seen court-appointed guardians play with some of my previous placements and that had often produced enlightening results.

'What's this?' she asked, eager to sit down and get stuck in. She loved it when she had me all to herself. I sat beside her with a bunch of colouring pens in my hand.

'Well, we're going to transform this piece of card into the ocean. And then we're going to create three islands. Will you help me draw them?'

She nodded vigorously, her eyes shining. Chewing her lips in concentration, she scanned the array of felt-tips, pulling out the colours she wanted to use. The tip of her tongue popped out in concentration as she worked and when the islands were drawn she diligently added palm trees, sandy beaches, even a few beach huts. I coloured around her circles in blue, smiling at the sound of her humming. When she wasn't swearing and making threats to kill, she could really be a very sweet child.

'Done!' she exclaimed, 15 minutes later. She looked really proud of herself. 'Now what?'

'Now we use the Plasticine to make models.'

'Yay!' she cheered. 'Like dinosaurs and stuff? Or other animals?'

I shook my head. 'No, what I'd like you to do is make a model of everyone you know.'

Her face dropped in disappointment.

'It's OK, you can make some animals afterwards if you like, but let's do the people you know first.'

'Yay!' She reached for the yellow strips first and got to work creating faces. Craft was a wonderful escape for Phoebe; she became so absorbed in what she was doing that she barely raised her head for over 20 minutes. When she had finished she lined the models up in a row: first herself, then her mum and dad, Emily, Jamie and me, my mum and her teacher, Miss Angel.

'That's fabulous, Phoebe! Though you could have made me look prettier,' I nudged her teasingly with my shoulder.

'I gave you big yellow hair, though. Look!'

'I can see that, cheeky!' I laughed. 'Now comes the really fun part – the people get to travel and live on the islands.'

'Which one?'

'That's up to you. How many islands are there?'

'Three,' she said in a superior tone, rolling her eyes. 'That's so obvious, Rosie.'

'Right. So, one island belongs to you. It's your island and you are the chief so you get to say who lives there with you.

Where do you think you'd like to live? It can be one of the islands on either side but not the one in the middle.'

Phoebe reached for the model of herself and 'walked' it onto the card, pursing her lips in concentration. 'Hmm, I can't choose.' She sashayed her model across the page and back again, finally settling for the island on the left, the one with the sandiest beach.

'OK, that's good. Now we have to make a bridge.' I picked up a strip of Plasticine and laid it between 'her' island and the one in the middle. She shook her head in disgust, snatching it up and moulding a much more ornate creation, finally resting it in the same place as before.

'Great! Now, the people living on the middle island are allowed to cross the bridge and visit you on your island. But the people over here,' I said, pointing to the one on the right, furthest from Phoebe's, 'they can't ever visit your island, unless you build them a boat. So, come on, let's give everyone else a home.' I pointed to the models all lined up next to the card. 'Choose who you would like to live with you on your island, then you can put everyone else where you think they belong.'

She smiled, enjoying herself. 'I get to pick, all on my own?'

I nodded. 'It's all up to you – you're the chief. As long as you choose whomever you want. You mustn't worry about upsetting anybody, that's the only rule.'

'Can you pass Jamie, you and Emily over, please?'

She sat Emily and Jamie beside herself on the beach and

placed the model of me on the grassy part of her island, several inches away.

'Emily and Jamie are building sandcastles with me.'

'Right. So what am I doing?'

'You're about to go in the hut and do the washing up.'

I laughed out loud. 'That sounds about right! Now, you still have Nanny, Miss Angel, Mummy and Daddy left.'

She reached across me and scooped all of the models up in her hands. Without hesitation she laid them on the middle island then carefully separated the squished-up bodies before sitting them next to each other on the grass.

'Well done! So now everyone has a home,' I said, trying to disguise my disappointment. All Phoebe had done was re-create her present situation; the game hadn't revealed anything about the way she was feeling. 'And we can all visit each other by going across the bridge.'

She stared at me and frowned then shook her head. 'No,' she said. 'I'm not finished yet.'

Carefully she picked up the model of Miss Angel and held it by the head. At first she swung it towards the island furthest from her own then moved it back to the middle one again, frowning. She had seemed fond of her teacher and so such lengthy deliberations puzzled me.

'Having trouble deciding?' I prompted, wondering whether she felt her teacher had let her down in some way. 'You've dangled Miss Angel for so long her neck has turned into a noodle!'

Phoebe chuckled. 'I do like her,' she said slowly, 'but she didn't listen when I told her about the noise.'

My ears pricked up. It was the second time she had mentioned a noise. 'Well, I'd really like to hear about it. Will you tell me?'

She shook her head, decisively placing Miss Angel back beside her father on the middle island. 'No need – I don't hear it any more.'

I made a move to clear the game away, vaguely remembering from my research that tinnitus is sometimes an associated symptom of autism. I wondered whether Phoebe might benefit from wearing a special device to mask the noise, if it ever became a problem for her.

Phoebe flattened her hands on the card. 'I'm still not finished, Rosie.'

She reached down and picked up the model of her mother, holding the figure up in front of her. Suddenly she plunged it onto the edge of the card, the part we had coloured blue. Forming a fist, she ground the model down hard until it was no more than a flattened blob. Her face twisted with satisfaction, as if the model were an effigy that she could inflict pain upon using magical powers.

'Oh! What's happened to Mummy?'

'She's in the sea, being gobbled up by all the sharks – they're going to bite her face off.'

Chapter 19

Every day for the next week Phoebe asked to play the island game. She seemed to derive huge pleasure from being the chief, in control of all that happened and being able to decide everyone's fate for herself. Her most favourite part of the game was conjuring the destiny of the figures; her mother always met a sticky end. Most of the time Mummy got ravaged by sharks or bitten to death by jellyfish but occasionally she was condemned to living alone on the uninhabited island with no boat or bridge 'and definitely no sun cream, Rosie'. As the week went on the scenarios grew ever more elaborate: Phoebe even asked for extra Plasticine so she could model fire-breathing dragons and hungry, fierce dinosaurs 'to keep sun-burnt Mummy company'.

By the time the weekend arrived I put the game away at the back of the cupboard, worried that I might be fuelling some sort of sadistic pleasure in her. She wasn't impressed at all, announcing that she had had 'some more ideas' about what could happen to Mummy on the island. It was certainly interesting that she felt so much anger towards her mother. I wondered if it was because it was she who had hurt Phoebe's arm and caused her to come into care. She didn't seem to harbour any anger towards her father; he was able to cross the bridge whenever he liked, although he was never allowed to live with us on 'her' island.

'Please, Rosie, p-l-ease. I want to build a bonfire on the island.'

Oh goodness, I thought, now she wants to burn Mummy to death. 'No, we've finished with that game – we'll play Fall Guy if you like.' Fall Guy was a trust-building game where Phoebe was supposed to stand in front of us with her eyes closed and her arms in the air. She would then fall backwards and had to trust one of us to catch her.

'OK.'

She was definitely getting better. At first she stood stock-still, hardly daring to move. With lots of encouragement she would fake a fall and stumble, shooting her own arms behind her, ready to support herself if we let her down. Now she was able to keep her body flat and drop backwards but still she couldn't bring herself to keep her eyes closed.

With the arrival of Jamie she dropped me like a stone. Lately he had taken to lying in and at weekends only emerged from his room after nine. From the moment she got up, usually around 6am, she would bug me to wake him.

'Jamie! Shall we play in the garden?'

'Yep, if you like.' My son was still playing it cool but he loved being in demand. Phoebe looked delighted. She raced off to get her pirate dress on while Jamie ate a hurried bowl of cereal without even sitting down.

As I sat watching them chasing each other around, I wondered whether she would remember the times when she had been happy with us. Since her arrival there had been moments of high tension and misery, but she had laughed lots as well. There was also an unmistakeable bond forming between her and Jamie. I hoped it would give her the confidence to form friendships with her peers, something that didn't seem to have happened for her in the past.

She was certainly capable of forming positive relationships, which was a good sign. And the more 'brain training' we did, the more convinced I became that Phoebe was in the wrong school. With a bit more help I was confident she could be transferred into mainstream education.

The sound of the doorbell broke my thoughts. My heart flew into my mouth when I opened the door to a figure robed from head to foot in black, a pair of eyes staring out at me through a small slit. My first thought was that Phoebe's parents had sent someone to snatch her back – I had been confronted on my doorstep by desperate parents before, as well as at the school gates. I always kept my mobile phone close to hand, usually in the pocket of a cardigan or in my jeans, so that I could call 999 at the first sign of trouble.

Fingering the keys of my handset, I was debating whether to slam the door and put the security chain on when I spotted a local authority ID tag with the name

Nabila Hussain attached to the robe. Relaxing, I noticed a gentleness around the eyes that had evaded me in my panic and realised the visitor wasn't a threat – it was actually a woman dressed in a burka.

'Oh hello,' I said, slight suspicion still lingering in my tone. 'Can I help?'

The woman removed the veil covering her face. 'I've come to collect Phoebe for contact.'

'She doesn't have contact today,' I said, though even as I spoke I was already doubtful. It wasn't unusual for contact arrangements to be bungled, but usually it was a case of contact supervisors forgetting to collect children, rather than the other way around. Unwilling to send Phoebe off with someone I'd never met before, I asked the lady to come in and wait while I checked her credentials with the contact team. They confirmed that a meeting with her parents had been arranged and that Nabila was a bona fide contact supervisor.

After calling Phoebe in from the garden I apologised to Nabila.

'Sorry about that – I wasn't expecting anyone to collect Phoebe today. You can't be too careful.'

Nabila gave me a curt nod, clearly none too impressed by my caution.

Phoebe bounded in, closely followed by Jamie. When I told her she was going for contact I was surprised to see a flicker of disappointment; I thought she would be keen to see her parents – well, her father at least. 'Run up and get changed now, Nabila's waiting.'

'Can't I stay like this, Rosie? I want to show Daddy my dress.'

'Hmm, I don't think so. You'd best put something smart on.' When children went on contact visits the parents often scrutinised them, hoping to deflect attention from their own failings by accusing others of neglect.

Nabila tutted and gave me a look of annoyance, clearly upset at being kept waiting any longer.

'Oh, OK, I suppose you can. Let me do your hair quickly then.' I ran the brush through her hair several times, still amazed at how luxuriant it was becoming. 'There. All done.'

Phoebe left with a silent, unsmiling Nabila, looking a little unsure. It had unsettled her when I had explained that I wouldn't be allowed to supervise her contact sessions any more and I could tell she was uncomfortable with going off with a stranger. I saw her off at the door with a reassuring wave. 'Have a lovely time, honey.'

I was still annoyed with social services. Through the years of dealing with them I had come to expect ineptitude; in fact it was a total surprise when things actually ran smoothly. Whenever I complained about their disorganisation I was met with a general malaise. Sometimes it felt as if the children they were busy removing meant no more to them than mere names on a report. I wondered whether many of them actually cared about the welfare of the youngsters they were legally responsible for.

Chapter 20

Phoebe returned from contact in a highly agitated state, her eyes burning feverishly. It had been days since I had seen her so upset and so I was a bit thrown off-kilter, unsure of how to deal with her. Every time I asked what she had done during the hour she spent with her parents she either repeated the question back to me or made unpleasant screeching noises.

When Emily got home from her regular two-hour stint at the local charity shop I suggested that she and Jamie choose a DVD to watch while I took Phoebe out into the garden. Jamie fired a dozen questions at me but Emily had the sensitivity to agree without any fuss, throwing a knowing look over her shoulder as I led Phoebe outside.

The sun was bright and so I headed straight for the swing, settling beneath its shade. Seated at one end, I patted the middle cushion next to mine and Phoebe took the space in silence, leaning back into its quiet haven.

'Everything OK at contact?'

Phoebe shrugged, kicking her legs so vigorously that the swing swayed from side to side instead of back and forth.

'I can tell you're having a difficult day, sweetie. Do you want to tell me why?'

Her legs stopped mid-swing. She huffed, throwing herself at me in a sort of aggressive hug. Elbows first, she followed with her head, burrowing into my chest. Biting my lip to suppress a yelp, I put my arm around her, guiding her into a gentler hug.

'I wanted you to come,' she growled, her face twisting around to fix me with an accusatory glare. Her eyes had a sunken, defeated look about them. She continued to grind her elbows aggressively into my chest.

'I know, honey. But you still got to see Mummy and Daddy, didn't you?'

She gave a tiny nod before burying her face in my tummy. Over the next few minutes her breathing grew louder and louder. It sounded as if she'd been running, even though she had hardly moved. After a moment I realised that she was hyperventilating and my stomach pitched and rolled with the expectation of what she might be building up to.

'If I tell you a secret, will you promise not to tell anyone?'

I clenched my jaw, knowing my answer might scare her into silence. It was tempting to tell her a white lie, just to get her talking, but I knew that in the long run it would have ruined the trust between us.

'I'm sorry, honey, I can't do that – I might have to tell Lenke. But I do promise to keep you safe, whatever you tell me.' At that moment I cursed her social worker for being a virtual stranger to her, certainly not someone who had inspired her with confidence. All of the muscles in my body tensed as I willed her to talk to me.

'I don't like it when he hurts me,' she said eventually, gasping with the effort of releasing the words.

I felt a renewed thrashing sensation in my tummy but breathed it away, trying to impersonate someone calm and professional. 'Who hurts you?' I asked tentatively, knowing how careful I had to be. If she were capable of expressing exactly what she had been through, enough for a criminal investigation to be launched, any conversation I had with her would count for nothing if it were believed that I had taken the lead in any way. As foster carers we were only supposed to listen and record disclosures. Questioning a child in any detail was forbidden and only carried out by experienced Child Protection Officers.

She sat up, her expression haunted. 'The man – I hear the man coming up the stairs and then the noise starts.'

'What man? What noise?'

She crawled away then, as if physically trying to escape from the conversation. Crouching in the corner of the swing, she covered her face with her hands. Clearly she wasn't ready to reveal her tormentor, but already I assumed it was her father. An image of Robin Steadman came to mind, the embodiment of success with his expensive watches and immaculately pressed suits. It was difficult to marry his cool composure with the greasy, ragged picture I had always conjured of child abusers.

I waited to see if she would say any more but after a moment I realised she wasn't going to. She was crying softly into her hands, her shoulders trembling as the sobs grew harder. Reaching out, I bridged the gulf between us by gently touching her shoulder. It was a gesture I hoped would convey solidarity as well as comfort.

'How did he hurt you?' I asked as the sobs subsided into little hiccups. Reaching into my pocket, I pulled out some tissues and handed them to her. Palming them flat in both hands, she covered her face and breathed, slower now, into the tissues.

'When I … he hurts me … in my bed. And … I'm in the bath … sometimes when …'

Her whole body trembled as she spoke, the words jumbled in broken sentences. Though I was tempted to pull her into a hug and say, hush, don't try to speak, I knew that the pain had to come out and putting it into words was the only way, however difficult it was for her to do so. I sat motionless, concentrating on the movement of clothes on the line in an effort to keep my expression bland.

She began sobbing again, hiding her face in her hands. 'Don't look at me!' she snapped when I turned to her, so I stared straight ahead, feigning interest in the flowering shrubs in a colourful array of pots around the deck. There were several minutes between each sentence when all I could hear was the sound of her sobs, but I didn't try to rush her and made no further attempt at comfort either, in case she took it as a sign that I had heard enough.

'I wanted it to stop. I told him how much it hurt but he put his hands over my mouth and told me to be quiet.' Her despairing voice jabbed at my heart.

Lowering her hands, she risked a glance in my direction.

'And the man makes the noise?'

She shook her head. 'No, I think it's my ears that make the noise but then I have to make a bigger noise to make the nasty one go away.'

I nodded slowly, filled with a deep yearning to give her a cuddle. I wondered whether it was possible for a child to be so frightened that the wiring in their brain could misfire and cause tinnitus. It was another mystery to investigate using Google, as soon as I had the time.

Forcing a grim smile, I pressed gently ahead. 'What did he look like, this man?'

She was looking at me but her eyes were unfocussed, exhausted now with the effort of trying to find the words to explain an act that was completely beyond her understanding. As the minutes passed I tried rephrasing the question in several different ways but nothing drew a response. Her whole body seemed to deflate. As the sun lowered I decided not to probe any more. Part of me wanted to grab her by the shoulders and ask if it was her father who had hurt her, but that would be too suggestive and so I said nothing.

When we made our way back inside it was as if Phoebe had aged a few years. Her shoulders sagged and her feet shuffled lethargically. Again she reminded me of an old lady in a nursing home. No wonder, I thought, with the burden she's been carrying around with her. And then, with a nauseous sinking in my stomach, I wondered just how long she'd been living with it.

Until recently I had thought that the placement was about to end and Phoebe would be going home in a better state than when she arrived. My hands were shaking as I prepared tea, trying to absorb the realisation that, far from being over, the nightmare for Phoebe might have only just begun.

Now the protective walls she had surrounded herself with were gradually dismantling there was no telling what other revelations might be unleashed.

Chapter 21

When I called Lenke the next morning to report Phoebe's disclosure, her tone filled me with the unmistakeable sense that something was wrong. Launching into a summary of our veiled conversation on the swing, I got the distinct impression that the social worker was not fully concentrating on what I was saying. Surely she appreciated the gravity of the situation by now?

When I fell silent there was a pause before she sighed. 'OK, record everything and email it to me.'

Why is it I feel like I'm being a nuisance? I wondered.

'Hmm, the thing is, Rosie …'

Another hesitation.

'There has been a complaint. I need to contact your supervising social worker and come along to interview you.'

My heart plummeted. 'What complaint?'

Phoebe came in from the garden and plunged onto the sofa, screeching loudly. To block out the row I pressed a flat palm against my right ear, concentrating so that I could make out what the social worker was saying.

'I can't tell you that at the moment. Are you free later today for a visit?'

So you can find the time to come and see us now, I thought acidly, knowing she would only divulge the nature of the complaint in person, so that I wouldn't have time to cook up a story. It was standard procedure but I couldn't help but feel resentment towards her. Where were her visits when we had needed some advice? 'Yes, I'll make sure I am,' I choked, my mouth dry. Already my stomach was churning. I wanted to meet her as soon as possible, so that I could find out exactly what I was dealing with.

'Good. The legal team have been informed – I'll be seeking their advice before I come. See you later, Rosie.'

A dark thought occurred to me.

Swallowing hard, I couldn't free the grip of tension in my throat as I ended the call. With the legal team involved, there was no telling how serious the complaint might be. I knew from training that children who had suffered sexual abuse could sometimes misinterpret an innocent gesture as something threatening, confused by their earlier experiences. Surely Phoebe hadn't made an allegation against me, had she?

It was impossible to concentrate for the rest of the day as I racked my brain, trying to work out what I could possibly have done wrong. A number of possibilities came to mind, one being the incident with the scissors. I knew her parents were unhappy that Phoebe had got hold of a sharp instrument. Maybe they'd waited until now to make a formal complaint? It was impossible to know for sure and as the hours passed, though I kept myself busy making sure that all my financial records and daily diaries were up to date, I grew more and more anxious.

By the time I answered the door to Desmond late that afternoon, I had already decided that I needed to cry. I could feel the threat of tears rising but knew I must keep a lid on it until the children were in bed. I was grateful for the continuing dry weather; Jamie and Phoebe were in the garden and could stay there out of earshot, until the dreaded meeting was over with.

Desmond's cheerful smile faded in concern at the sight of me. 'Oh dear, you's catastrophising again. Come on, let's make you a cuppa.'

It was true that I was prone to fearing that the worst thing possible was likely to happen. And the most awful allegation I could possibly think of was to be accused of sexual abuse. I could imagine no greater horror and although the fear had never been strong enough to prevent me from fostering, it had always been a niggling worry at the back of my mind.

'Rosie, whatever it is, it cannae be that bad. The parents are trying to muddy the waters because they're shocked at the direction things are going in. It's probably no' a direct accusation from Phoebe.'

'I know you're probably right.'

'Well, tell your face that, then – you look terrified.'

With a superficial calm I answered the door to Lenke. Bypassing pleasantries, she gave me a curt nod and swept past me into the hall. Following behind, I was relieved that Des was there to offer her a drink and keep the atmosphere genial.

Without waiting for Des to bring her tea, she launched straight into business, her tone already reproachful; her manner intense. 'Where do you buy Phoebe's clothes, Rosie?'

'Sorry?' Even as I spoke I had a horrible feeling I knew what she was getting at. Des walked in, handed Lenke a steaming mug then leaned against the doorway, his face a picture of puzzlement. He had no idea where this was going but, by then, I did.

She cleared her throat. 'Phoebe's clothes – can you tell me where you take her to buy them?' The floral blouse she wore did nothing to soften her expression, leaden with gravitas.

'Look, if this is about the pirate dress I can explain …'

She interrupted me before I could continue. 'You know, of course, that part of the payment you receive each week must be spent on clothes for Phoebe. *New* clothes.'

'Yes, but this was in addition to her normal clothes – a present.'

She shook her head from side to side. 'So you think that because she's a Looked After Child, she doesn't deserve new presents?'

I was annoyed by her attitude but I remained calm. 'Of course not, and I've bought her lots of new things since she came here. It's just that we were passing the charity shop and she fell in love with this particular outfit.'

'So you should have found out where it came from and bought her a new one. Her parents are very upset about this. They say not only was Phoebe dressed in old clothes but she was also unkempt and dirty. They have made a formal complaint, questioning your standards of care, and now we have all sorts of extra paperwork to deal with.' She was staring at me as if I were on trial for some grievous crime, and feeling like I was back at school and summoned by the headmistress, I found myself floundering for an appropriate response that wasn't sarcastic.

I wasn't surprised that the Steadmans had complained; most parents were prepared to fight dirty if they felt under threat of losing their child. I wondered whether I would do the same if I found myself in the parents' situation, but then I quickly dismissed the idea. If Emily and Jamie, when they were younger, had been sent to stay with complete strangers, I would have done all I could to try and build a positive relationship, knowing that the children would be at the mercy of their carers.

Sadly, rogue foster carers do exist and when parents were prepared to risk alienating those who were responsible for the children's welfare, it made me wonder just how loving they really were. Usually I tried to rise above petty grievances and not take them personally but given the state of Phoebe's hair when she first arrived, I felt it was a bit rich for the Steadmans to complain about hygiene and standards of care.

What I wanted to tell Lenke was that worrying about what the girl was wearing and ignoring the carnage in her mind struck me as just a little bit twisted. Of course, I didn't say that. Over the years of fostering there have been many times when I have longed to speak my mind but have kept quiet through a love of my job. I wondered whether one day my self-control would falter and it would all come tumbling out in front of some unsuspecting social worker. For now, though, I sat in silence as I swallowed down the tirade and so was immensely grateful to hear Des's strident voice.

'Rosie chose to spend her own money on a second-hand item. Surely that's a matter for her and no one else?'

Before Lenke could respond, Des answered his own question. 'If her financial records are up to date and all the relevant allowances have been passed on, there's nothing else to be said.' He remained as genial as ever but there was a finality to his tone as he told her that he was sure lessons had been learnt. He finished by saying, a tad facetiously, that all purchases would be made from approved retailers from now on.

After checking my financial records, which were thankfully now up to date and showing that I had overspent on clothes for Phoebe, Lenke gathered her things together. With a slight prickliness she rose to leave, assuring us before she went that from the answers I'd given to the questionnaire, Phoebe had amassed enough points to qualify her for an assessment from a CAMHS counsellor. It was a relief to know that she would have someone with some professional knowledge to talk to. Though I tried my best, I really had no idea whether the responses I had given Phoebe were the right ones, or even if there was a right way.

Des stayed for dinner and once Phoebe was in bed and Emily and Jamie were sprawled out in front of the TV, we sat at the dining table sipping coçoa. He had read a copy of my report but I ran through Phoebe's disclosure again, as much to share the burden of it as anything else. 'She hasn't named her abuser yet,' I added, 'though it's pretty obvious who it is.'

'Hey, that's not very open-minded,' he said in mock-chastisement.

'I know, but who else would have had the opportunity?'

'Do you really need to ask me tha', Rosie? Don't be so naive. Look at some of your other placements – teachers, babysitters, ministers even. It could be anyone. And she hasn't actually said what's happened yet, has she? Not specifically. She did seem low, though, at dinner. Far more subdued than when I last visited.'

Should I bear some responsibility for that? I wondered. On some level, perhaps I was partly to blame. I felt like I should have done a better job than I had. It was undeniable that the child was in a worse state after the period in my care than she had been in when she arrived. 'Perhaps the burden of protecting her abuser's identity secret is wearing her down?' I suggested.

Desmond pursed his lips. 'Mmm, perhaps. Naming him will certainly reduce the power he has over her.'

The pressure of the day finally got to me and I hunched my shoulders, biting my lower lip to hold back the tears. Des must have noticed the strain in my face. He reached across the table and touched my cheek with the pad of his thumb. The kind gesture only made me more choked.

'Rosie, it's OK. I'm here, let it go.'

It was tempting. Des was someone I could imagine myself coming to rely on and I certainly felt like I could do with the comfort, but I brushed him away and rose to my feet. 'I'll be OK after a hot bath. Come on, it's late – Mrs D will be expecting you at home.'

He smiled, though he looked slightly offended. 'If you're sure you're OK.'

A bath brought me to the point of no return and the tears began to roll. I indulged them, telling myself there were some things so terrible that the only natural reaction was to cry and there was no doubt that, by anyone's standards, Phoebe's history warranted someone to cry for the loss of her childhood.

It was difficult to believe that she had slipped through the net for so many years, with no one suspecting there might be a more sinister reason for her strange behaviour than autism. I knew that many of her symptoms could be put down to her condition but I couldn't help but wonder why she hadn't felt able to disclose what she'd been through, until she came to me. What we had done for

Phoebe wasn't special in any way – aside from offering her a stable, loving, calm environment – and I certainly wasn't qualified to deliver any sort of therapy. I suspected that she was beginning to open up because for the first time in her young life, she felt safe. How could so many people, her parents, teachers, even medical staff, have failed her?

It didn't matter how many disclosures of abuse I had listened to since becoming a foster carer, each time was as bad and shocking as the last. But there was something in this case that disturbed me more than ever before, though I couldn't, for the life of me, think what it was.

Chapter 22

The display on my bedside clock read 2.24am when I finally decided to give up chasing sleep. There was a clatter of metal as I threw back my duvet and switched on the light. At first I froze, wondering if Phoebe was up to something dangerous again, then I realised it was probably the sound of a scavenging fox in one of the neighbours' dustbins.

Since the self-harming incident I had been alert to threat, waking at the tiniest of sounds. Pausing, I listened carefully, only switching on the television when I was sure everyone was safely in bed. After watching BBC News 24 until the same headlines rolled round again I flicked through various channels, unable to find anything that grabbed my interest enough to chase away my fears about what horrors Phoebe might have endured.

Restless, I ran my fingers through the books on my shelf and made a listless attempt to engage my brain by flicking through my old favourites, but again, I found it impossible to concentrate. My head was too full of Phoebe and now even her father was strutting around my mind with impunity.

Still wide-awake two hours later, I was so deep in thought that the alarm, when it went off, threw me into a spin of panic and made my stomach roll. Mechanically, I showered and dressed, my thoughts continually returning to Phoebe. Something definitely didn't feel right. I just wished I could gain her trust enough to find out exactly what it was.

At breakfast Phoebe sat at the dining table, staring blankly ahead. An untouched plate of toast and jam was on the table in front of her, as well as the obligatory porridge with grated chocolate on top. When I prompted her to eat she picked up the spoon and twirled it in the bowl, tracing swirls in the chocolate but making no attempt to put it anywhere near her mouth. It was heartbreaking to see her so desolate and frustrating too. There was something deeply disturbing about seeing a child in a depressed state but I felt helpless to do anything about it.

When Emily and Jamie came downstairs and sat at the table she barely even raised her downturned eyes. They gave her quizzical looks but said nothing. Their own expressions were miserable, feeding off the gloom. The silence was unnerving so I switched on the radio and began washing up the breakfast things, clanging cups and bowls clumsily to inject some life into the house.

Staring out of the kitchen window and across the garden, I remembered how lifeless four-year-old Freya had been when she first came to live with us in 2003. After several disclosures she seemed to sink further into her own gloom, but months later she had made what seemed to be a full recovery. I was surprised to see how quickly she became well, but maybe it had helped that she was so young.

On Radio 2 Vanessa Feltz was interviewing a man who had been unable to leave his house for the past 30 years because of the mountain of rubbish he'd hoarded, half a lifetime's work. He cheerfully confided to the presenter that none of it would have been possible were it not for obliging family members delivering food and other essentials through the narrow gap in his hallway.

Seven years of fostering had taught me how much damage loved ones could inflict on their own flesh and blood. I watched Phoebe as she gazed lifelessly out of the window, wondering whether it was her own closest relatives that had caused her so much hurt.

Chapter 23

As I climbed the concrete stairs of the local authority offices the next day I was filled with a feeling of disquiet. The navy blue walls and peeling paintwork didn't create the most welcoming environment. But it wasn't the grimness that made me feel uncomfortable; it was the anticipation of what lay ahead.

It was never easy to sit opposite birth parents at a Looked After Children's, or LAC, Review and tell them uncomfortable truths, but somehow it felt all the more difficult when those parents were as articulate and well-bred as the Steadmans. LAC Reviews are meetings held regularly to provide updates to all professionals involved in the case and to discuss the child's care plan. As well as the foster carer and child's parents, school teachers, health professionals and sometimes police officers attend the reviews.

Up on the second floor I passed several notice boards, one with a poster pinned on it with the wording 'EVERY

CHILD DESERVES A LOVING FAMILY' followed in a smaller font by 'Could You Adopt an Older Child?' I wondered if it would come to that with Phoebe. And if it did, would a family welcome her permanently, with the severity of her problems? If not, she could stay with me; I would be her safety net. But at that moment, I reminded myself as I knocked on the third door to the right, she still had two apparently loving parents. Could it be that they were all that they seemed and someone else was responsible for taking a bright, trusting young girl and breaking her?

Dust-ridden aluminium blinds hung at the window of the small meeting room. The walls were a drab off-white and the cream carpet was stained. Most of the space was taken up by a scratched conference table, surrounded by eight grey metal chairs, two of them occupied. Lenke looked up and gave me a brief smile. Next to her sat Juliette Worth, the chairwoman. I had met her at several other reviews. She was a no-nonsense middle-aged woman with a plain face and a strong Yorkshire accent. 'How are you, Rosie?' she beamed when she saw me. 'Nice to see you …' I got the feeling she was going to say 'looking so well', but being a Northern woman she couldn't bring herself to flattery when it wasn't due and left the rest of her sentence floating in the air.

It appeared that Mr and Mrs Steadman had arrived just before me. They stood together on the far side of the room, their shiny selves incongruous against such a dreary backdrop. Phillipa, her expression pinched, sat and planted her neat handbag gently at her feet, while Robin edged around the table to offer me his hand. He met my eyes, smiling affably, and I wondered how he felt with the tables turned on him. In his job, it was usually he who got to say what was what.

'Hello again, Rosie.' Robin spoke in a tone someone might use with a much-loved relative. It was impossible not to respond pleasantly to his natural, effortless warmth and I shook his hand with a firmness equalling his own. I took a seat opposite the couple, watching them carefully. Phillipa sat wringing her hands, her whole body language exuding unease. It wasn't surprising, I thought, considering what the pair of them were going through.

Strange then that her husband should appear so unrattled by recent events, as if he had absolutely nothing to worry about. Dressed in a crisp navy blue suit and striped satin tie, Robin Steadman leaned back in his chair and as he cast a laconic eye around the room it was easy to picture him wooing high net worth clients and making deals at the click of a finger.

After sweeping around the table with formal introductions, Lenke distributed copies of the agenda and summarised the events that had led to Phoebe being taken into police protection, touching on the local authority's reasons for applying for an ICO (Interim Care Order). Juliette read out a report from the school, their feedback being that Phoebe's behaviour had been much more erratic of late, swinging from excellent concentration to violent temper tantrums several times during each school day.

A slight, smug smile brushed Robin's lips on hearing the teacher's summary and he nodded in a knowing way at Juliette, satisfied by the evidence that Phoebe wasn't doing as well in my care as she had at home.

'And so, Rosie, perhaps you could tell us how Phoebe's coping at the moment?'

'She is quite low, I'm afraid.' I paused and glanced at Lenke – it was so difficult to judge exactly how candid I should be, although I got the sense that this wasn't the right time to understate Phoebe's despair.

'Why do you think that is, Rosie?' Lenke asked in a pointed way, presumably giving the go-ahead for frankness.

'Why do *you* think it is?' Robin shot out, his tone unfailingly polite but with a definite angry undercurrent to his words. 'It's quite obvious I would have thought – she's desperate to come home. The girl doesn't know where to turn, she's so confused.'

'We'll come to you in a moment,' Juliette said, holding her hand up towards him and continuing to smile at me.

'She's opening up a bit about her past experiences,' I said, gaining momentum under the chairwoman's encouragement. 'I think it's difficult for her to cope with the feelings that her memories are provoking.'

'What memories?' Robin asked crisply.

Lenke jumped in. 'Phoebe has grown to trust Rosie. She's confided a number of worrying things in her over the past few days. Nothing specific but we have reason to suspect some sort of abuse.'

I was impressed by the social worker's demeanour. She was noticeably cool but still professional. It seemed that she had finally accepted that abuse knows no boundaries.

Phillipa looked startled. Indignation flooded her petite features so suddenly that her face and neck were awash with colour. Robin narrowed his eyes in distrust. From their reaction, I gathered that Lenke hadn't told either of them anything about Phoebe's disclosures. Robin's expression showed disbelief but he wasn't horror-struck, unlike his wife. He appeared to be a man confronted with news that was simply too ludicrous to take seriously. His confidence was so absolute that although it had been only a few days since Phoebe's disclosure I was already wondering whether it was indeed possible that she had made it all up. It was possible, of course, that there was someone else lurking in the background, someone the Steadmans trusted around their daughter. That is the trouble with abusers, I thought with a shudder: often they hide behind a veil of decency, expertly gaining the trust of family members.

'What ideas have you been putting in her head? It's funny how none of this arose until she went into your care,' Phillipa spat. 'You don't even dress her properly,' she added hatefully.

Unprepared for a return to what, in the current circumstances, seemed to me to be a particularly trivial complaint, I felt myself stiffen.

'We have photographic evidence that Phoebe is not being kept clean,' Robin offered, still using a conciliatory tone. It was as if he were suggesting pleasant destinations for a summer holiday rather than throwing out insults about my standards of care. 'Her shoes were scuffed during our last contact and she was dressed in an inappropriate, charity shop outfit.'

Phillipa's face wrinkled in disgust, presumably at the very thought of second-hand clothes. An image of Phoebe's matted hair came to mind and I could not help but raise a wry eyebrow. 'You have to appreciate that her last contact was sprung on me. If I'd had more warning …'

'We don't *have* to appreciate anything …' Robin interrupted, finally losing his cool. 'What you've done is taken a vulnerable child and twisted her mind with lies, trying to poison her against us.'

I swallowed. 'That's not true,' I said, feeling uneasy.

Juliette held up her hands, taking charge. 'Can you give us some idea of what she's been saying? Are we talking emotional abuse or …?'

'I guess it's partly emotional abuse she's describing but …' I was straying into dangerous territory and was unsure how candid I was expected to be. Again I glanced at Lenke. Was I going to have to recount Phoebe's disclosure verbatim? She nodded further encouragement. Without allowing myself to indulge the detail or embellish any facts, I began to relay our conversation as dispassionately as I could. 'Phoebe has indicated that a man has hurt her …' Unsettled by the look on Robin's face, I slowed down, taking a few deep breaths before continuing. 'She says this has happened in the bath and also in the bedroom.'

As soon as the words left my lips there was a throttled silence, the kind where the walls of the room seemed to close in, amplifying the tension through the air.

'That's a disgusting lie,' Phillipa spat, her chest rising and falling rapidly with the energy of resentment raging within her small frame. 'Why are you so bent on destroying this family?'

It was then that husband and wife exchanged the briefest of looks, betraying a vein of disagreement. There was something in the glance that set off an alarm in my mind. Just a small tone, barely more than a faint jingle, but there all the same.

'I would question your ability to interrogate a child. Are you qualified in any way?' Robin's voice dripped with sincerity but that only made it all the more sinister.

I gave him a penetrating look, hoping that it portrayed every opinion I had of him. 'I'm a good listener, Mr Steadman, that's all.'

There was another silence, more uncomfortable than the last, where it felt like all the air had been sucked from the room. A tension entered the meeting that was almost unbearable, particularly for someone like me, who would prefer to stay silent in a room full of people.

'This is all a terrible misunderstanding,' Robin protested eventually, but there was unmistakeable fear in his eyes. Lenke recognised it too. I could tell by the fleeting shadow that fell across her face, the way her eyes lingered on him for a moment longer than they should.

Distraught, Phillipa stood up abruptly, her chair thrown over by the backs of her knees. Robin also rose, simple surprise on his face as he watched his wife fumble for her handbag and stumble across the room. Self-assured though he was, the odd flicker in his face belied the fact that he had found the meeting, if not as unbearable as his wife had, at least fairly uncomfortable.

'You will be hearing from my company's firm of solicitors,' Robin said. When he spoke his manner, in contrast to that of his wife, was perfectly amiable. Still utterly in control, the momentary lapse in his composure forgotten, it was almost as if it could have been a figment of my imagination. 'When an ICO is in place the local authority shares joint parental responsibility with us, as her parents. You are therefore obliged to keep us informed of anything significant. You've been derelict in your duty and I shall be lodging a complaint against you, Lenke, for incompetence in dealing with us and keeping us informed about the welfare of our own daughter.'

Lenke was apparently impervious to insult, exhibiting no emotion other than serenity. Aware of the tremor in my own body, I felt a grudging respect emerge for the social worker. She appeared completely calm, merely blinking in response to the atmospheric change in the room. No doubt she was accustomed to the sort of scene erupting before our eyes, but my heart was beating so fast the movement was visible through the thin material of my T-shirt.

Thankfully it had been a long time since I had faced animosity as absolute as the Steadmans'.

Chapter 24

For the first time since I registered, I was seriously beginning to wonder whether I should ever have become a foster carer. From as early as I could remember it was all I had wanted to do. My early employment, after leaving school, had simply been a means to an end, a way of earning a living. No career had appealed to me like fostering had and somehow I knew, from a young age, that it was something I would one day do. Of course there had been moments over the past few years when I had had wobbles, particularly in the stressful early days of a placement, but on the whole I loved caring for children and I cherished the idea of it; of making a difference and doing something meaningful.

But as I sat hunched in front of my computer at 5am, the morning after the LAC Review, writing a report justifying my reasons for buying a second-hand outfit, I realised that sometimes, being a foster carer was less about making the lives of children better and more about covering your own back. I was able to embrace political correctness up to a point, in so far as it helped to reduce racism and other forms of discrimination, but in some cases it was a poisoned chalice.

My eyes were raw from the recent sleepless nights and I closed them for a moment, swinging around on the chair to face the window. It was tipping it down outside and although it wasn't that cold, goose bumps were visible on my arms. I felt an inner chill that had nothing to do with the weather. Robin Steadman had invaded my thoughts again. I was no expert in psychology but I was convinced there was something not quite right with his body language at the LAC Review – in fact his whole demeanour had seemed off.

Without prior warning, he had received the news that his daughter may have been abused, possibly sexually. He was told that her attempts to confide this information had left her depressed and withdrawn. Surely any father ought to have been distressed, angry, bewildered, or even numb? Bearing in mind how close they seemed to be, I would have expected any reaction other than passivity.

My daily diaries were spread out on the desk in front of me. Once my report was complete I needed to fill in the diary entry for the previous day. After a complaint I knew how important it was to keep detailed, accurate notes but for a while I just sat watching the rain strumming against the window, the bleak greyness of our rain-lashed street invading every corner of the room.

Emily and Jamie got up at 6.30am. With Phoebe still in bed they seemed a bit more cheerful than they had of late, bickering in a jovial way over who was going to have the last of the chocolate cereal. By the time they left the house at 8am, I still hadn't managed to get Phoebe up.

Every 10 minutes I had gone into her room and tried stirring her into action but so far, nothing had worked. The rain had cleared and so I had even tried opening the window, the fresh light breeze carrying the scent of freshly mown grass into the room. Sunlight was burning hazily through the clouds and streamed in through the open curtains but still she lay listlessly in her bed, oblivious to it all, curled on her side in the foetal position.

'Come on, Phoebe, you'll miss school at this rate. They're doing cookery as well, so Miss Angel tells me – jam tarts. I've got all the ingredients ready for you.'

But her eyes remained fixed on the wall, she didn't even turn her head to acknowledge me. Reaching for *Harry Potter and the Philosopher's Stone*, her favourite book at that time, I started reading, hoping to gain her interest enough to get her moving, or at least interacting with me in some way. It didn't work. Refusing to turn around and look at me, she pulled the duvet up to her chin and closed her eyes.

'OK, you can stay off school today if you're not feeling up to it, just this once. So, what would you like to do? Shall we go to the park?'

She shook her head. Even that small movement seemed to be more effort than she could manage.

'Come on, let's think of somewhere – I'll take you anywhere you want to go.'

Every suggestion I made was met with resistance, but she did finally agree to come for a drive. It wasn't what I'd hoped for but at least she got up and dressed, and it offered her a taste of fresh air, albeit for the few seconds it took to walk from the house and through the puddles to the car on the drive.

With the sun emerging it was warming up so we drove along with the windows wound down. With no destination in mind I switched unconsciously to autopilot and so we ended up heading out of town, whipping past several new housing developments. I slowed as the roads grew narrower, shops and residential streets giving way to rolling fields and farmhouses. Overhanging branches from woodland trees shielded the sun from view.

We passed a row of neat white cottages and in the forested distance a deer warning sign. I braked in case a fawn should dart out in front of us and glanced in the rear-view mirror, about to tell Phoebe to look out for one. When I saw her expression I swallowed my words, knowing nothing was likely to catch her interest: she looked absolutely vacant. I thought she might react when the wheels bumped over a cattle grid but she barely blinked, even when I told her that a rabbit had sprinted out from the undergrowth and stood on hind legs in the middle of the road, the sun glinting off its silver fur.

After about half an hour I pulled into a lay-by just past a hand-painted sign for a farm food shop and opened the driver's door. A roux of fresh earth, pine and forest flowers drifted in through the gap. 'Shall we go for a walk across the fields, Phoebe? There's a church just over the hill – can you see the spire? They have a tea shop and …'

'Nooooo,' she said. It was more of a wail than a stubborn protest.

I swung around to look at her. Her face had come to life and was full of anguish.

'Don't look at me, Rosie. Stop looking at me.'

Turning back, I rested my elbows on the steering wheel and rubbed my hands down my face, staying that way for several moments. Eventually I slipped the key back in the ignition and was about to fire up the engine when a small, stricken voice from the back made me freeze.

'Why did the man do it?'

'Do what, honey?'

'Hurt me.'

How could I possibly explain to a nine-year-old the reason some humans were capable of depravity, when I couldn't begin to understand it myself? 'Sometimes adults do bad things,' was all I came up with. 'None of it was your fault, Phoebe,' I said gently. 'The man should never have hurt you – it was wrong.'

With a brief glance in the rear-view mirror, I could see that she had begun to cry. Silent tears rolled down her cheeks. I longed to comfort her.

'Can I come into the back with you, sweetie?'

'Nooo,' she wailed again.

'OK, it's alright. I'll stay right here.' I knew that over the years many children in care had made disclosures during car journeys. Tucked away, out of view, it was a safe way for a child to reveal something shocking without the pressure of being watched or judged. Children were often so fearful of being disbelieved that they couldn't bear to witness the effect their words would have.

She began to shake, convulsions gripping her thin frame. Instinct told me that we were close to full disclosure; all I needed to do was to wait and let it come. After a few minutes she began retching. It sounded as though she was struggling for breath. My eyes shot to the mirror again to make sure she wasn't choking.

'He puts it in my mouth,' she sobbed, her face twisting and convulsing with disgust. She looked as if she might actually be sick. 'I can't breathe when he does it, Rosie. I can't breathe.' She gasped for air and shook uncontrollably, as if the pain of the memories was as fresh as the day they took place.

My stomach was seized with revulsion. I was struck by the realisation that this was another of those moments that would stay lodged in my mind forever, however much I tried to overwrite it. Feeling sick to my stomach and hardly wanting to continue myself, I kept my eyes fixed on a pile of freshly sawn logs at the end of the lay-by, the concentration helping me to keep an even tone.

'I'm so sorry you had to go through that, sweetie. That shouldn't happen to any child.'

My seemingly calm reaction must have had some effect because when she next spoke it was with less reluctance, the words tumbling over themselves in her eagerness to get them out. 'And he sometimes puts it down there.' In the rear-view mirror I could see her arm moving. With a rush of nausea I guessed where she was pointing. 'That's when it stings the most. He gets cross when I make a noise so I cry in my head when he does it.'

Her sobs became loud and racking. There was a click as she released her seatbelt, drawing her legs up to her chest and resting her face on her knees. After five minutes of continuous crying I could bear it no longer. Turning slowly, I pulled the door release and went to climb out. She needed to know I was on her side and I felt an overwhelming urge to hold her.

'No, please, Rosie, stay there.'

In the glove compartment there was a pack of tissues. I reached over and plucked a few from the top, then dangled them over the back of my head. She took them and gave an exhausted blow of her nose. 'I need more,' she managed to choke out, all her sinuses full and her throat clogged with mucous.

We stayed like that for what felt like an age, Phoebe sobbing into her soggy tissues and me sitting helplessly a few feet in front of her. Gradually the sobbing subsided and all I could hear was her breathing, heavy and muffled with her nose so blocked. 'The man isn't always mean,' she said, after a further five minutes of silence. 'Sometimes he's nice. I think he must really be two different people – do you think he might be?' she asked in a tiny and what I sensed was a somewhat hopeful voice.

'Hmmm,' I said, trying to sound as if I thought that might be possible.

Another few minutes elapsed while I willed her to continue. When she didn't say any more I decided to risk a prompt.

'What is his name? The mean man?'

'He hasn't got a name – I just call him *horrible man*.'

She fell silent again. I thought carefully about how to continue. After a while I asked, 'How about the nice man?'

'Huh?' She hiccoughed through her sobs.

'What do you call the man when he's being nice?'

A pause. My jaw was beginning to ache through clenching it so tight.

After a few more sobs she choked, 'Daddy.'

When she spoke the low hum of a tractor engine from across the fields and the shouts of children playing in the distance seemed to recede. All I could hear was Phoebe's tremulous voice repeating itself over and over: *Daddy, daddy, daddy*.

An overwhelming swell of sadness rolled through me as she dissolved into a fresh outburst of sobs. I felt such deep sorrow for her. Without caring whether she objected or not, I reached for the door handle and released it. Suddenly light-headed, I steadied myself by gripping the frame. Grabbing the precious few seconds of fresh air, I took some deep breaths then climbed into the back and sat beside her. She sank down to rest her head on my lap.

'You'll be alright, you know,' I soothed, stroking her damp hair. 'Everything will be alright.'

The high voice I heard didn't sound like my own.

'When am I next seeing Daddy?' she asked in a small voice as we walked into the house a while later.

Her face was still red and swollen, large blotches covering both cheeks. There was a long pause while I weighed up what I should say to her. There was no way I wanted her to feel guilty for what she had revealed, but at the same time I felt I had to be honest. It was no use making false promises. 'Well, I'm not sure yet, honey. We'll need to talk to Lenke and decide the best thing to do.'

Panic filled her eyes, fresh tears following in its wake. 'I lied about that stuff.' She flapped her arms as if the gesture would be enough to make it all go away. 'Daddy didn't do anything, Rosie, he didn't hurt me – I was pretending.'

She was sobbing now, her thin hand gripping mine so tightly it was beginning to hurt. A tight ball of anger unfurled itself in my stomach. How could any man bring himself to hurt a child in such a vile way? I wrapped my arms around her and held her close, stroking her hair and making shushing noises. That was almost the most shocking thing of all: the love children have for their parents, no matter what harm has been visited on them. 'I know it's hard, sweetie. But the most important thing to us is that we keep you safe.'

Gripping hold of my cardigan with both hands, she buried her face in my chest, crying and crying. Steering her to the sofa, I sat down and she flopped next to me, her whole body racked with sobs. We stayed like that for what felt like an hour, her head buried in my shoulder while I patted and stroked her back. She trembled so violently that I was worried for a moment that she might go into a fit, but still I didn't move, wanting her to express her grief, and knowing it had to come out, one way or another.

When she eventually fell silent I turned my head slowly, my neck stiff with the weight of her leaning against me. I was surprised to find that she'd fallen into an exhausted sleep.

Chapter 25

Phoebe's disclosure was so shocking that when I woke the next morning I wondered for a moment if I'd dreamt it. I longed for 9am to arrive so that I could report it to Lenke and then give Des a call. When I had telephoned the out-of-hours duty social worker after Phoebe had gone to bed, her advice was to discuss the matter with Phoebe's own social worker in the morning. It felt wrong to do nothing but wait, as if I were ignoring an emergency situation, although I could appreciate that in the arena of social services what had happened to Phoebe wasn't that unusual.

It was at times like this that I felt totally disconnected from the real world, completely alone. Child abuse was hardly a subject I could bring up over a cup of tea with my next-door neighbours. To protect Phoebe's confidentiality I couldn't even share what I knew with my closest of friends. I wondered if this was how severely depressed people felt, drifting through each day with no one to turn to, no anchor to keep them from sinking.

Which was probably exactly how Phoebe was feeling. Overnight her life had changed. I wondered whether she was able to fully comprehend just how far-reaching the consequences would be. Never again would she be going home to both parents. If she were to go home, it would be to her mother, as a single parent.

She was deeply attached to her father and so it was a depressing thought. All night I hadn't been able to think of anything else and my stomach was still churning with the knowledge of what she'd had to endure. She hadn't given any indication as to how old she was when the abuse began, but from what she had said, I got the impression it had happened repeatedly.

As soon as I got up and pulled on my dressing gown I bypassed my usual pit stop at the kettle and ran straight into the bathroom, kneeling down on the bath mat and throwing up into the toilet bowl. Grabbing some tissue, I sank my head back against the wall and closed my eyes.

After a few minutes I pulled the flush lever and stood, washing my hands and splashing some cold water on my face. I just wanted to repeat what she'd said to someone, to tell them over and over to purge the knowledge of it from my brain. What I felt, I realised as I climbed into a hot shower, was unclean. Debased by the sickening images swimming around in my mind. No wonder Phoebe had ingested so many cleaning products, I realised, with a sudden bolt in my solar plexus; it was as I'd suspected – she was trying to clean herself from the inside out. Soap and water weren't enough to rid her of that awful feeling.

As I got dressed I suddenly remembered Phoebe telling me about the noises inside her head. It occurred to me that what she had been experiencing was a manifestation of utter panic whenever she sensed her father was planning a visit to her room. If only her teacher had been more attentive when she had tried to tell her about the noises, she may have been rescued from her abuser sooner. In some ways it was a blessing that her mother had lost her cool and struck out, injuring Phoebe's arm. If that hadn't happened, I realised with a shudder, she might have been trapped in a cycle of abuse for many years to come.

Phoebe hardly ate any breakfast again that morning and when I left her lined up in the playground she looked so pale I marvelled that she even had the energy to stand there. She appeared close to collapse. Was her catatonic state a manifestation of post-traumatic shock? I wondered, knowing school was probably the best place for her, to keep her mind distracted, although it was tempting to grab her hand and take her back home with me.

I spent the rest of the day feeling close to tears. Every sinew of me was overwhelmed by what Phoebe had said and it was difficult to concentrate on anything. I went through the motions, whizzing around the supermarket straight after the school run, then driving to our local children's centre to attend the formal foster carers' support group, but nothing stilled the emotions swirling around inside my head.

The group get-together was arranged by the local authority, the idea being that all of the borough's foster carers would convene once a month to discuss any concerns they might have and offer support to other carers who might be going through a difficult time. Although I was registered with an agency, it was still expected that I should attend all of the local authority training and workshop days. Monthly attendance was compulsory, but since it was an official coffee morning chaired by a social worker, it wasn't a relaxed experience and most of us remained tight-lipped, wary of moaning freely and then having everything we said rcported back to the fostering team manager.

Jenny, Rachel and Liz were all there when I arrived and I sat with them, but apart from exchanging pleasantries, we didn't say much except that we would try to get together for a meal sometime in the near future, if we could all coordinate our back-up carers to stand in for us on the same evening.

This particular meeting was chaired by Bridget, a black lady in her early forties who amazed us all by managing to appear with a different hairstyle every time we saw her; today she wore long braids twisted and piled high on top of her head. She was a cheerful woman, who seemed totally down-to-earth. I had got to know her quite well a couple of years earlier when she was social worker to one of the children in placement with me and she seemed to possess a discretion that ran deeper than her job required but still I wouldn't have opened up in front of her. Paranoia runs deep in most foster carers.

Bridget ran through the agenda for the day, one of the items being record taking. The social worker emphasised the importance of keeping accurate, meticulous notes as a way of avoiding complaints and allegations. I stifled a snort. My records were accurate but I still hadn't thought that buying Phoebe a dressing-up outfit was worthy of mention. And even if I had recorded it, the complaint would still have been made.

'Doesn't make a whole lot of bleedin' difference,' Pauline piped up from where she sat, in the corner of the room on a large purple beanbag. 'I lent my little un's buggy to a contact supervisor and she reported me after finding the head of a Jelly Baby stuck to one of the straps.'

Pauline was a Londoner who had moved up north years earlier. She had been fostering with the local authority for over 20 years and was one of the few who really didn't care who she upset. All she was interested in was the children and everyone else could 'go stuff 'emselves' as she put it.

'Well,' Bridget said, somewhat carefully, 'it serves to remind us to keep up our standards of care. You could use it as a learning tool, Pauline, to help you grow as a carer.'

'Grow as a carer?' Pauline's face reddened. Jenny, Rachel, Liz and I all exchanged smirks. 'Grow as a bleedin' carer? I bin fostering for over 20 years, Bridget! You show me a busy mum anywhere in the country who don't have bits of bleedin' Jelly Babies somewhere about the place. It'll be a mum that gets the nanny to take the kids out while she swans off to the ruddy gym.'

The rest of the meeting passed peacefully enough and although I hadn't said much, I felt slightly more cheerful when I left the children's centre and went home to do an hour's housework. I hadn't shared the news of Phoebe with anyone but the simple act of mixing with people who were experiencing emotions similar to my own was uplifting.

Later that day my mother came around. I hadn't been expecting her and was supervising Phoebe in the bathroom when Emily called up the stairs to say Grandma was in the kitchen. I had a feeling our earlier telephone conversation had prompted the unannounced visit; I had forced a cheery tone and made all the right noises about being fine but age hadn't watered down Mum's witch-like ability to sense upset in one of her children. Somehow she knew I was feeling the strain and she wasn't going to let me suffer alone.

She was waiting at the bottom of the stairs as I trudged down. 'Come on, I want to get home for *EastEnders*,' she said briskly, as if it was me who had insisted she interrupt her evening to come round and counsel me. Propelling me to the kitchen, she directed me to one of our high stools and patted her hands on my shoulders, the loving gesture releasing the emotions that I'd kept bottled up inside. My eyes welled up. Making a low clicking noise that said, '*Hmm, I knew it*,' she immediately switched the kettle on.

How funny, I thought, that she always turned to tea in turbulent times, as if the caffeine-filled leaves were a magical balm to soothe ragged nerves. Personally, I would have preferred her to slip me a dose of something more calming.

'How's Phoebe doing?' she asked in hushed tones. As was her way, she got straight to the heart of the matter. Emily and Jamie were back watching TV in the living room and Phoebe had asked if she could read quietly on her bed, something she had taken to doing over the past couple of days. I didn't think she would be able to hear us talking from up there but I was glad that Mum wasn't taking any chances.

For a few seconds I considered fobbing her off by glossing over all the details and telling her I'd just had a bit of a day of it. Forming the words somehow seemed too much of an effort and anyway, I knew I really shouldn't tell her anything; Phoebe's history was confidential. But, then again, she was my back-up carer. Foster carers aren't allowed to use unchecked babysitters – anyone left to care for fostered children must be screened by social services. My mother had attended a respite carers' course and been interviewed by the local authority, who had also checked her background. As one of Phoebe's carers, I reasoned that she should be included on the 'need to know' list. Few people possessed more discretion than my mother and besides she had a way of staring at me that rendered me incapable of keeping anything secret.

Once I started jabbering it all came out, along with a few tears. Mum listened in silence, raising her hand to her mouth when I told her about Phoebe's father.

'That poor, poor child,' she said quietly.

I nodded grimly. 'And now she's even more down than when you saw her the other day. I thought our talk might have helped her a bit, but,' I chewed the inside of my lip, 'she's so lifeless, as if all the energy has been shaken out of her.'

She shook her head and remained deep in thought for a few moments. It was peculiar but whenever I confided in Mum, all the physical symptoms of stress seemed to vanish from my system. My stomach, having churned constantly all day, suddenly settled. I felt as if I had handed part of Phoebe's distress to her, thereby sharing it. She sometimes drove me mad with her intuition and occasional disapproval, but she was a wise old bird and also had an amazingly calming effect on me. I was so deeply thankful for our relationship that I pitied all the children I'd known with tumultuous lives, who hadn't grown up in the certain knowledge that they were constantly welcome and wanted.

Filled with a sudden wave of affection, I leaned over and kissed her on the cheek.

'Thanks, Mum.'

'What for?'

My eyes filled again. 'Just, thanks.'

The kettle made faint hissing sounds. Steam rose from the spout and surrounded Mum's head like an aura. 'It's not surprising, love, with what it sounds like she's been through. Must have been horrific for her, the poor child.' Mum shook her head, the wrinkles in her forehead burrowing deeper into her skin. 'You can't expect her to reveal something of that magnitude and then be right as rain.'

'I know. I suppose I expected some change in her, some sort of relief after naming her abuser, but she seems worse than ever. I know the way she was in the early days was exhausting but at least she was full of life. Makes you wonder where it's all going to end.' I sighed. 'I'm not sure I'm up to dealing with all of this.'

'Hmmm.' Mum blew over the hot liquid in her cup, then, wrinkling her nose, she took a tentative sip. Her glasses steamed up in the process. 'You've just got to get on with it and do the best you can,' she said. Being a war baby, it was her standard mantra when times got tough, and one I was used to hearing. 'All you can do is wait and see which way the wind blows.'

She paused, pulling her glasses off and cleaning them with the edge of her blouse. When she put them back on she pushed the frame further up the bridge of her nose with her forefinger and squinted at me. 'I'm sorry to say this, love, but perhaps there's more to come.'

Chapter 26

Over the next couple of days, Phoebe resembled a ghost as she wandered around the house, her alabaster complexion shocking me every time I walked into the same room. It was also unsettling to find her so utterly compliant: there were no protests, no tantrums. She did exactly as I asked of her without a single complaint. Her hair, though lustrous with all the attention and conditioner I had lavished on it, only amplified the colourlessness of her skin. There was a residue of shock in her eyes, their glassy stillness conveying such vulnerability that I just wanted to wrap her up and hold her, anything to break her out of her morbid reverie.

I wondered if her dream-like state was her mind's way of protecting itself, defensively shutting down all but the necessary processes. Her father's betrayal had injured her body but also her mind and it was my theory that his assaults, however long they had been going on, had triggered her descent into mental illness. From our conversations, I still hadn't managed to glean what age she was when he first began the abuse, but I suspected it was early on. Perhaps she would always have developed autism – I had no way of proving otherwise – but I suspected that the abuse had moved her way down the spectrum, drastically exacerbating her condition.

On one level, I reasoned, maybe this was a glimmer of good news. If abuse had made her illness worse, then surely freeing herself by talking about it would have the opposite effect? Before her disclosure I had witnessed a dramatic reduction in the strange movements and weird gait as she walked, the result, I thought, of being moved to a safe environment. She no longer felt the need to repel untrustworthy adults with alarming behaviour. There was no doubt that bringing the abuse to the forefront of her mind had caused a downward mental spiral but I hoped that by releasing the harrowing memories she would finally let go of some of the trauma that accompanied them.

I hadn't told Emily or Jamie any of the details of her disclosure but they could sense there had been a breakthrough of some sort. As far as I was concerned they deserved some sort of award for the renewed effort they put in with her, inviting her to play board games or offering up their electronic gadgets. I had said there was a problem with Phoebe's father and I think Emily immediately put two and two together. Jamie, though usually like a dog with a bone, didn't question me further, so perhaps he had an idea about what had happened as well. Either that or he preferred not to know. It wasn't to remain a secret for much longer anyway.

As was often the case, Phoebe began to confide in them. Youngsters often find it easier to talk to their peers, one of the reasons why the children of foster carers grow up fast. At first she revealed small nuggets of information, which Emily and Jamie would then relay to me but by the end of the week she was discussing her history openly in front of us all while watching TV, in the car, or, most often, at the dinner table. It turned out Mum had been right about the floodgates. Once they creaked open there was no stemming the flow.

Her openness took its toll on all of us, proving a double-edged sword. I wanted her to feel secure enough to tell us anything, and clearly she did, but there was a limit to what I wanted Jamie to hear. With Emily it wasn't as bad since she was older, but I worried about the effect Phoebe's talk would have on my son.

I was also anxious about the effect it had on her. With each confession, rather than showing some sense of relief, her mood seemed to grow darker. After school she would immediately change into her pyjamas and lie on the sofa or the rug, not wanting to move. Eventually even Jamie's invitations to play Wii fell on deaf ears. Lenke assured me that Phoebe's name was on the waiting list for counselling but I regularly pressured her to try and hurry things along.

As the long summer holidays neared I was hoping for a fundamental shift in her mood. As a family the six weeks away from the usual routine was our most favourite time of year. I loved the children being off, especially now they were older and we could visit different places without worrying about all the paraphernalia that comes with taking young children out.

A few weeks before the end of the summer term, we sat at the dinner table discussing options for our holiday. Jamie suggested camping but Emily's plans were more ambitious.

'We could rent a cottage in France or Italy. Aisha's going to Lake Garda next week – I'm soooo jealous!'

'Hmmm, not sure our finances would stretch to that,' I said, plus we didn't have a passport for Phoebe. Also I wasn't sure that I was confident enough to take her so far away from home in her current state of mind. As foster carers we were entitled to two weeks' leave a year, when any children in placement could be moved to another carer, but so far I hadn't taken advantage of it. It seemed unfair to ship Phoebe off when she would probably love a holiday as much as we would. 'I was thinking more of a cottage in Norfolk or something. We could invite Nanny, if you like?'

'Boring!' Jamie rolled his eyes. 'I want to go snowboarding or canoeing.'

'What do you think, Phoebe?'

She gave a heavy sigh. 'I don't like holidays.'

'Why not?' I had a feeling that the answer wouldn't be that palatable.

'When we go on holiday Daddy always gives me a bath. The noises follow me everywhere – he hurts me lots of times.'

We all froze, still shocked even though we'd heard it many times by then. Jamie held his fork in mid-air and Emily lowered her gaze to her plate, unsure of how to react. As Jamie had almost finished his dinner, I asked if he would mind taking his plate out and then going out to get the washing from the line. He hesitated for a moment, disgusted and yet captivated at the same time. A wave of my hand and a slight nod of my head got him moving. Emily watched us carefully, her face a picture of intrigue.

'Em, would you make a start on the dishes?' I piped up.

She looked as though she might protest, but I gave her a look and she started clearing the plates, piling them in the crook of her elbow.

Unprompted, Phoebe dropped her spoon back into the untouched bowl of porridge in front of her and told me that her father sometimes inserted objects inside of her. It was an effort not to gasp. I managed to suppress my horror but what I wasn't so good at was keeping my facial expressions under control. My ex-husband always said I had a plate-glass forehead and it seemed Phoebe could read my thoughts too.

'Why do you look so upset, Rosie?'

Annoyed with myself, I rubbed my hands up and down my face as if physically trying to erase my revulsion. But then, I thought, perhaps there were times when it was best to be honest.

'Because I *am* upset, sweetie – it's a good thing that you've told me and you're very brave but I'm sad that you had to go through that. No mummy wants to think of a child being hurt that badly.'

'Why doesn't *my* mummy get upset then?'

Chapter 27

Phoebe spoke without a shred of self-pity, as if her mother had supported her father in chastising her over some everyday event, like blaming her unfairly for breaking a vase or spilling her drink on the carpet, rather than being complicit in incestuous rape.

'Does Mummy know that Daddy hurts you then?' I knew it was a leading question but my thoughts were reeling, so much so that following the correct procedure went out of the window.

She nodded, picking up the end of her spoon and absentmindedly twirling her cold porridge around in the bowl.

'How does she know?'

When I heard her answer it felt like a physical blow.

'She watches.'

She said it simply, as if what she said was not unimaginably awful.

'Mummy says that all little girls have it done and I shouldn't moan about it or tell anyone or Daddy won't love me any more.'

Stunned was almost too mild a word for the way I was feeling. It was as if a syringe of ice water had been injected directly into my chest; the cold feeling spread through my stomach and down into my legs. Suddenly the smell of cooked vegetables lingering in the room became intolerable, winding its way into my throat and setting off a fresh spasm of nausea that left me feeling physically weak. My face reddened and I realised I was holding my breath. Phoebe noticed.

'You look like you're going to cry. Please don't cry, Rosie.'

So much for autistic children being unable to read facial expressions.

'I'm not going to cry, honey. I'm just sad, that's all. And cross, but not with you.'

'Why cross?'

'Because it's not true – little girls shouldn't have that done to them. It's wrong and Mummy and Daddy have done something very bad.'

For the first time in the conversation her face crumpled. She looked stricken.

'It's not your fault, sweetie,' I said quickly, reaching out and squeezing the hand that was resting in her lap. 'You've done nothing wrong.'

After a few beats she got up and walked lethargically over to me, leaning her weight against my side. Pushing my chair out, I held out my arms and she sat on my lap. When I encircled her in an embrace she leaned back, resting her head in the crook of my elbow like a young baby. I hoped she couldn't feel the panicked thrumming of my heart against my chest as she lay there.

It wasn't as if I'd never heard of a woman aiding a man in abusing children, but somehow I'd dismissed the possibility of ever coming across it myself. Any woman capable of a crime so hideous would chill me as deeply as the black-and-white speckled prints of Myra Hindley always had, surely? And yet I had sat at the same table as Phillipa Steadman. I had even, I thought, with a fresh spinning in my stomach, shaken her hand. The thought disgusted me. How had I not seen what she was? I was angry, remembering that I'd even felt sorry for her when Phoebe lashed out at her in the pizza parlour and then I remembered with a rush of guilt that I had thought Phoebe was behaving like a spoilt brat.

I took deep breaths to calm my racing thoughts, trying to order them linearly so that I had a better chance of accurately recording what Phoebe had said. If the case went to court my diaries might form part of the prosecution's case. Precise information was vital and it would be best to note down our conversations verbatim.

After a while her eyelids drooped and so I roused her, suggesting she go and lie on the sofa for a while. She was all too willing to get into her pyjamas – I think there was a certain security in knowing the unconsciousness of sleep lay not too far away – and she said she would prefer to lie on her own bed. Her eagerness to remove herself from our company worried me but, if I'm honest, I felt an overwhelming need to distance myself from her and so I agreed.

While she rested I sat at the computer and tried to record everything she had said as accurately as I possibly could. Emily brought me a cup of coffee, setting it in front of me and silently kissing the top of my head. When my report was complete, I emailed a copy to Lenke and copied Des in too, hoping he would call as soon as he read it. Once again I felt a compulsion to discuss it with someone, to reduce the impact Phoebe's words had on me.

Shutting down the computer, I stood at the bottom of the stairs, listening for any sounds of movement. There was nothing. I returned 15 minutes later but it was still silent so I quickly climbed the stairs two at a time and tiptoed across the hall, peering around the door to check on her. Remarkably, Phoebe lay unscathed after a conversation that had left me in shreds. Her quilt was thrown to one side and her dark outline stretched out in what appeared to be a relaxed posture.

As I stood watching her, terrible images of what she'd told me catapulted themselves into my brain again. If this was what it felt like just to have knowledge of her history, what on earth must it have been like to live through it? I couldn't help but wonder what scenes replayed in her mind when the lights went out. No wonder the poor child woke up screaming in the night. But there she was, all her bodily organs functioning as they should – lungs breathing air, heart pumping oxygen around her system.

Despite everything, she was surviving. I marvelled then at the resilience of the human spirit.

Chapter 28

Over the next couple of weeks Phoebe's mood circled, going from depression to fury until exhaustion, then spinning back to a lethargic low. For me the frustrating thing was that the violent outbursts or sessions of prolonged, loud wailing would occur out of the blue, just when I thought we were making some progress towards recovery. Each episode would be followed by yet another disclosure, though none could have shocked me more than when she told me that her mother had taken a role, albeit a passive one, in her sexual abuse. Although it was sickening to hear her stories, I hoped that by talking about the abuse she was changing the balance of power, taking the authority away from her abusers and thereby liberating herself.

Much of her anger was directed at me and I got the impression she blamed me in some way, perhaps for being the one who had finally prised her secrets out of her. She would kick out at me as I passed by, though never actually daring to make contact. I think the relationship we had built prevented her from taking a step too far and she knew I simply wouldn't tolerate it, but she would come dangerously close before swerving and inflicting her fury on a cupboard or piece of furniture.

It was a fair enough response, I reasoned. If she hadn't made any disclosures she would already have been back home with her mother and father. Even though the status quo was terrible, it was a horror that she knew well. There was a strange comfort in the familiar, even if the familiar was terrible abuse. Besides, most children have a fierce loyalty towards their parents, however undeserved it may be, and Phoebe was no exception. Lenke confirmed that contact with her parents was suspended, perhaps indefinitely, depending on what happened legally. Arrangements were being made for Phoebe to be interviewed by experienced police officers from the local Child Protection Team but I hadn't heard anything since a hurried telephone conversation with the social worker.

Telling Phoebe the news that she wouldn't be seeing her parents for the foreseeable future was a task that fell to me, but for several days I had been putting it off. Already she was struggling to come to terms with what I imagined she saw as her betrayal of them. It seemed brutal to twist the knife that bit further.

Phoebe tended to drift from day to day in a sort of 'not quite there' haze, with us working around her as best as we could. The only time when she seemed to be truly lucid was when she was in a rage. Watching her go through such turmoil was an emotional drain and we all felt it; even Emily and Jamie looked tired.

Getting her to school was an exhausting enough feat in itself. My own children would join in with the encouragement as I ran through all the exciting things she might get up to each day, trying to coax her into her uniform and out of the door. She would fold her arms and adopt that splayed legs pose of hers, the one that told us she wouldn't be going anywhere without a fight. The funny thing was I was certain that her refusal to comply had nothing to do with naughtiness or obstinacy – that would have been more easily dealt with. She seemed to be genuinely terrified of the place.

Some mornings she was so anxious about leaving the house that her whole body would tremble. Even the hair on her head shook if we got so far as the car on the driveway. Her nerves reached a climax as we approached the school gates and then, if we were lucky, she would calm slightly and plateau, at least enough for me to guide her into the playground. Her teachers, aware of the problem, made the concession that I should be allowed to line up with her and escort her into the classroom.

I think Phoebe's class teacher and some of the support staff felt ashamed once I had given them an overview of what she had endured at home. The knowledge that they had failed to respond to her attempts to reach out for help must have pained them, although the children they taught had such high levels of need that I knew it can't have been easy for them to provide individual care.

Accompanying her to the classroom seemed to help her a little but each time I made a move to leave she would cling to my arm and fix me with such a look of despair that I felt physically sick. Only after several 'cross my heart' promises that I would come back for her would she let me go.

Another Google search offered some enlightenment on her behaviour. I read about some parents who had been hauled through the court system, accused of allowing their children to truant. Some of the families claimed their child suffered from 'school phobia'. It seemed that children who had suffered loss or bereavement were most likely to develop separation anxiety, which in turn caused a fear of going to school. With all that Phoebe had been through and the sudden loss of her family, her fear of abandonment wasn't surprising; finding a name to tag onto the problem felt like a positive step forwards but I had a feeling that telling Phoebe the news about her parents would set us back even further.

Knowing I couldn't put it off any longer, I waited for a moment when Emily and Jamie were busy upstairs and then invited Phoebe to come and join me on the sofa for a chat. Her look was pensive, an anxious 'Oh no, what now?' expression, the sort that should never appear on the face of a child so young.

Tears streamed down her face as soon as I mentioned her parents, before I'd even revealed the news about contact. Holding her hand, I said, 'And so a wise man, called a judge, is going to decide when you're next going to see Mummy and Daddy. But the wise man is very busy and so it might take a little while before we find out what he thinks is best.'

Phoebe was beside herself. She wept, sobbing into my shoulder, her hands clinging onto my top so tightly that the knuckles went white. 'Can I just see Daddy quickly then? Just for a little while? Please, Rosie. *Please*! We could go to his office.' Her eyes were wide and panicked. 'I know where he works – we could go on a train. P-l-ease take me, Rosie.'

'Why is it you want to see Daddy but not Mummy?' I couldn't help myself; I had to ask the question that had been puzzling me since I first discovered her mother's complicity in the abuse – why Phoebe seemed able to forgive her father, when he was the actual perpetrator.

She stopped crying for a moment and, hiccupping, she managed, 'Daddy cuddles me.'

It was a simple statement but on hearing it I felt terribly, utterly sad. She loved her father, forgave him everything he had done to her, because somewhere in the midst of all the exploitation he had found time to give her a hug. A deep loathing ran through me and I wanted to tell her that the man didn't deserve her love; he didn't even have the right to breathe air, as far as I was concerned. I had to tune out of our conversation for a moment, allowing time for me to put my own feelings to one side. She continued to plead, using such a desperate tone that as I shook my head, I felt utterly wretched.

'I'm sorry, honey. It's not up to me. But I tell you what we can do. We could draw some pictures for Daddy, if you'd like? And maybe write him a letter?'

Her sobs subsided a little, comforted I think by the offer of some sort of contact, however indirect. I wasn't sure whether letter contact between them would even be allowed, but I reasoned putting her feelings down on paper couldn't do any harm and might actually be cathartic.

The day after giving Phoebe the news about contact I received a call from the school receptionist barely two hours after I had dropped her off. Apparently she was inconsolable, so much so that the teachers found it impossible to even talk to her. When I arrived, she was waiting alone outside the school office, her small frame swamped by the large blue sofa she was sitting on. She looked pale and tearful but her face brightened a little when she saw me.

I felt a stab of irritation at the staff for leaving her alone in such a vulnerable state. Although I knew that the receptionist was nearby and probably keeping an eye on her, no one was offering the vulnerable child any comfort. In the past I had found the children I looked after were lavished with attention and praise by sympathetic teachers but it seemed to me that Phoebe got a raw deal all ways round and appeared to be largely ignored.

A wave of wooziness hit me as I walked towards her and I wished that I had eaten something for breakfast. So much had happened over the past few weeks that I had completely lost my appetite, giddy with the emotion of it all. Anger had been my constant companion ever since Phoebe's first disclosure and yet there was no way of venting it. I longed for her father to be called to account for what he had done, but until that happened I had a nasty feeling that the injustice of it all would probably continue to eat away at me. Even my skin felt tender to the touch.

It broke my heart to see Phoebe so grief-stricken and as we left the building I started to wonder if there was any good in the world. The trouble with watching someone suffer so deeply, apart from the obvious anguish for the poor child, was that it shook my faith in human nature. I've always been a person who prefers to believe that tragedy strikes for a reason and ultimately everything works out for the best. Watching Phoebe in my rear-view mirror as I drove home, slumped as she was in the back of my car, it was near impossible to sustain that conviction.

Chapter 29

When we got home Phoebe changed straight into her pyjamas and laid herself out on the sofa, catatonic with hopelessness. I wondered whether the trauma of the last few weeks had actually triggered some sort of mental illness. Or, I ruminated, was her state a natural human response after experiencing such loss?

I telephoned Lenke and described Phoebe's despair, trying to drive home the need for urgent counselling. The social worker assured me that if an appointment was not forthcoming within a week, she would authorise me to arrange to see someone privately. It was a relief to know that professional help wasn't too far away.

The disclosure about the complicity of her mother in the abuse had, I think, triggered a deep sense of despair in Phoebe. Even as an adult I found it almost too unbelievable to comprehend that a mother was capable of such betrayal. The one person in the world that she should have been able to turn to for help was actually jointly responsible for violating her in the worst way imaginable. It wasn't any wonder that verbally acknowledging her cruelty caused so much suffering.

I had hoped that her admission all those weeks ago was the nadir of her misery. At the time it certainly felt like a major breakthrough but now I wasn't so sure. Back then I had thought that by exorcising her demons she would emerge, if not healed, then at least achieving some form of deliverance. Although I had heard the worst that a human being was capable of, I wasn't beyond holding out for a miracle.

Of course I realised that by releasing her secrets she wasn't going to be instantly better; she was deeply, perhaps irreversibly, traumatised. I also knew that, despite the occasional input from CAMHS, the task of helping her to move on and put the past behind her was down to me. In my head I visualised Phoebe in transition, stuck between night and day. What I wanted to do, what I was convinced I must do, was help her to starve her awful, dark memories of energy by crowding them out, filling her head with bright, happy thoughts instead.

It was an unrealistic theory, perhaps even childish, but as I watched her glassy eyes staring into space, there wasn't a whole lot more harm that could be done, I thought. The memories would always be horrific, but hopefully, after cramming her days with as many positive experiences as possible, she would be distanced from them, not so haunted.

For now I bustled around her as she half-dozed on the sofa, placing a small coffee table beside her and arranging a comic, a glass of Lucozade and a few snacks within arm's reach. It was something my own mother did for me whenever I was poorly as a child and I could remember how safe her tending made me feel. But with Phoebe my attempts to cheer her by fussing, even while I was doing it, seemed to me to be pathetically inadequate, like trying to stick a plaster over a gunshot wound. In truth, I really didn't know what else to do. Over the last few days I had tried to avoid asking her 'Are you OK?', because clearly she wasn't and I knew the question was probably just a reminder of all her troubles.

But ignoring her suffering and simply hoping it would go away wasn't helping either. Heartbreak was inevitable after what she had been through, what she was *still* going through. There were no shortcuts: she had to face her loss and get through it, just as an adult must confront grief. When there was no more room on the side table for my offerings I perched myself on the edge of the sofa and leaned over her.

I chose my words carefully, knowing that whatever I said could not possibly make any of it better. 'Phoebe, I know you probably aren't feeling that strong at the moment but this is the last time that you're going to sleep during the daytime, OK?' I wasn't going to be able to take her pain away, but it occurred to me that there might be a way to influence how she viewed it. I could only pray that my bumbling would do more good than harm.

She said nothing. Her eyes, ringed with dark circles, remained fixed on the ceiling. I cleared my throat, wondering how to get the message across that the only way to get through the pain was to take it one day at a time, screening the bigger picture from view.

'From now on, when you're feeling weak and tired, we're going to keep busy instead of lying down,' I said, grappling for some ideas as I spoke. 'We're going to make bookmarks and candle holders.' I don't know why I came out with that, but then again, it really didn't matter what she did so long as she kept busy and there was some sense of purpose there, something to work towards. I knew that in the darkest moments of life, routine was a safety net that offered refuge from panic and feelings of helplessness.

I had made the discovery years earlier when in the throes of divorce.

Trying to build a new life for myself while hiding my misery from the children hadn't been easy and the only way I coped with the first few months of adjustment was by breaking each day into small chunks. Hours at a time, and as each day passed, I rewarded myself with some small treat, mainly chocolate (though sometimes something stronger). But I found that as the weeks passed the groups of hours increased and soon whole days went by without me even thinking about it. Structure had certainly kept despair at bay. Phoebe's suffering was obviously something far worse, but it was the only way I knew how to try and help her cope.

We sat in silence for several minutes but then she turned her head towards me.

'What things are we going to make?'

Although it was clearly an effort for her even to talk to me, there was a glimmer of interest in her tired gaze. It was the first real sense I got that, with time, the vortex of misery might just slow itself down.

Chapter 30

'What's so special about you that you think you deserve a charmed life while the rest of us suffer?' It was another one of my mother's sayings that she rolled off her tongue when things got tough and as the days passed I found myself repeating it over and over. I never thought I'd say it but her no-nonsense philosophy really did seem to be a useful strategy to get through each day and avoid getting dragged down by Phoebe's low moods.

On a positive note, it had been four and a half days since her last violent outburst. The trouble was, she replaced her tantrums with silence, so most of the time we barely heard anything from her. When Phoebe was home and Emily and Jamie were busy, either at school or with their friends, she stayed sullenly by my side. Apart from trips to the bathroom, when she would wait outside the door, calling out to me every few seconds to make sure I was there, she rarely strayed more than a few feet away from me.

On the days when I hadn't managed to coax her to school we sometimes went a whole hour without saying a word to each other, but it was a companionable silence. I've always been more of a listener than one of life's talkers. Whenever I'm conscious a constant stream of monologue goes on inside my head but most of the time I don't feel the need to share it and, bizarrely, even though she had barely ever been quiet during the first few months she spent with us, I got the impression that Phoebe was the same.

On the days when she did make it to school it wasn't unusual for the receptionist to call halfway through the morning to say that Phoebe had reached meltdown and needed collecting. Although I knew it was best for her to stay in a structured environment, I no longer dreaded Phoebe being sent home. I was surprised to find that I actually enjoyed our peaceful afternoons together.

She had given up pleading to go to bed in the middle of the day. At first I'd felt mean when I refused to allow her to change into her pyjamas and regularly questioned whether I was doing the right thing, but after a few days she accepted that I meant what I said and so learnt to shake off the tiredness by doing other things.

Sometimes we sat side by side on the sofa, flicking through a glossy home interiors magazine, or we worked together in the garden, preparing the vegetable patch for planting or tidying the borders. One day at the beginning of July 2009, with the school holidays fast approaching, Lenke called to let me know that the local Child Protection Team were ready to interview and asked whether I could escort Phoebe to the local authority offices the next day. Although relieved to hear that it had been decided not to put her through the trauma of a forensic medical examination (so much time had elapsed that the procedure was unlikely to provide physical evidence of assault), I worried about how she would cope with what I imagined would be intensive questioning.

It was one of those days when Phoebe had barely managed an hour at school before they called me to collect her, and now she sat curled up on the sofa reading a book. I decided not to mention the police interview until the morning; the less time she had to fret over it, the better. Already my stomach was working itself up into a frenzy so I figured I was doing enough worrying for the both of us.

On arrival at the interview suite my nerves were immediately calmed when we were greeted by a smiling, plain-clothed police officer in her early thirties who introduced herself as Helen. She was dressed in a floral top, flowing black skirt that almost reached her ankles and sparkly flip-flops. Her informal attire seemed to reduce the magnitude of the occasion and I hoped that Phoebe felt the same, although she had barely uttered a word to me since breakfast, when I had told her where we were going.

I also hoped that the interview wouldn't be a repeat of our visit to see the CAMHS psychologist the previous week, when Phoebe had sat sullenly in the corner of the room refusing to engage, not even to join the doctor in colouring in a picture. Helen's cheerful banter as we followed her to the first vacant interview room inspired some degree of confidence, however, although the expression on Phoebe's face when she saw the video equipment told me otherwise. There were a few boxes of toys and books on the floor beside a central table but they did little to lighten the austerity of the room.

Unable to be party to the interview in case I steered her testimony in some way, I waited outside, straining my ears to see if I could hear what was being said. By the time the door reopened about 40 minutes later my palms were stinging from clenching my fists so tightly. I'd been willing her to cooperate, desperate for the police to reach a position where they were able to take action against her parents.

If the angle of Phoebe's obstinately protruding chin hadn't given away that disappointment loomed, then Helen's pursed lips and a small shake of her head certainly confirmed it.

'I don't think Phoebe is in the mood for talking today, I'm afraid.'

My heart sank. With no physical evidence of abuse, Phoebe's testimony was crucial. My notes alone, I had already been told, were not substantive enough to bring a case against her parents. While there was little doubt that there was enough evidence to secure a Full Care Order for Phoebe, a criminal prosecution hung in the balance. I knew that few child abusers were successfully prosecuted for their crimes and the thought that the Steadmans would get off scot-free made me sick to my stomach.

Standing, I gestured for Phoebe to try out the rocking horse at the end of the waiting room and then went to speak to Helen.

'All I could get out of her was that she slept in the loft extension at home, which goes along with the classic scenario.'

I frowned, not following. Helen explained that it was common for parents to place an abused child in a room furthest from the front door, so that passers-by or unannounced visitors wouldn't be able to hear their distress. I shuddered at the thought.

'But apart from that I got absolutely nowhere, I'm afraid. She just kept repeating everything I said.'

Typical Phoebe. I rolled my eyes. 'Oh no, I'm sorry.'

Helen leaned closer. 'It was really bloody irritating, between you and me.'

I laughed. 'Yes, don't I know it? Do you think we could try again another day? If she gets to know you first, maybe she'll open up. Or, if not, could I ask the questions and a police officer film it covertly?'

Even before Helen shook her head I knew I was clutching at straws. If the case was to stand up in court, there were procedures to follow, I knew that, but I just felt there must be some way of seeing justice done. I think Helen sensed and shared my frustration. She squeezed my arm and told me all was not lost – 'There are other ways to skin a chicken.'

Immediately intrigued, I was disappointed not to be able to probe further, since Phoebe had grown tired of the horse and was back at my side, pulling on my arm and moaning that she was tired and needed to go home. As we left Helen tapped her lip with the pad of her index finger and assured me she would be in touch.

By the time we got home I wasn't sure who was more exhausted: Phoebe or me. It was awful to think of a child so young having to go through the ordeal of being questioned and the sunken look to her eyes gave away what an effort it had been for her. The phone was ringing as we stepped over the threshold. As I answered the call Phoebe brushed past me. As soon as her shoes were off, she lay down on the sofa and closed her eyes.

It was Phoebe's court guardian, Linda, a lively woman in her early 50s who had represented some of my previous placements. As is usual when the local authority is seeking a Care Order, the court had appointed an independent person to be the voice of the child, supplying the judge with recommendations that would be in the child's best interests. I updated Linda on the latest situation, including Phoebe's reluctance to cooperate with the police. Although she was supposed to take an objective view, I could sense she shared my frustration.

She told me that she had already visited Phoebe on a couple of occasions at school but had met with the same blank refusal to talk to her and so was struggling to get a sense of the child's viewpoint. I was surprised to hear that they'd already met and was slightly annoyed. It was important, I felt, that as Phoebe's carer, I should be kept informed of those sorts of visits. Even though she hadn't cooperated with her guardian, being quizzed about her feelings towards her parents must have been upsetting for her, particularly in the school environment, where she would have been pulled out of lessons for the purpose. I wondered whether her visits had coincided with Phoebe's panic attacks at school. It wasn't any wonder that I had found it difficult to identify the triggers of Phoebe's moods and tantrums when I wasn't armed with all the information.

Linda promised to keep in touch and provide me with regular updates on the progress of the case, something I was grateful for since I doubted that Lenke would bother. Walking back into the living room, I perched on the edge of the sofa. I wanted to try and stop Phoebe sleeping if I could – she needed a good night's rest after what she'd been through – but I wasn't going to try too hard, not today. It was possible that her brain needed to switch off after all the drama.

'We *need* to make a start on those bookmarks,' I suggested in enthusiastic tones. Liz, my foster carer friend and ex-head teacher, had told me that whenever she wanted a child to follow a command she always used the word 'need' instead of 'should' or 'can'. She assured me that most children would respond if they were told they 'needed' to act – it was something to do with the power of suggestion.

It often worked and this time was no exception. Phoebe sat up and yawned, stretching her arms above her head.

'OK.'

When I had told Emily of my latest ploy to try and stir Phoebe from despondency by getting her to make things, my inventive daughter had come up with the idea of trying to sell what she made at a car boot sale. Phoebe, though she lacked interest in most things, had seemed to like the idea.

She followed me to the table and, caught by surprise, I bustled around gathering pieces of card and paintbrushes, trying to hurry before she lost what enthusiasm she had managed to muster. For the next hour we sat side by side, carefully ruling lines on the card and then cutting to make small rectangles.

Phoebe's efforts were half-hearted at first, but once she'd produced her first bookmark and witnessed my reaction (I heaped so much praise on her on seeing the end result that anyone looking through the window might have thought she'd presented me with a winning lottery ticket) she was eager to do more, even embarking on two at a time. I couldn't help but smile as I watched her; she was so absorbed and worked with such care. I hoped that the activity quelled the upset that must have been churning inside her and that the temporary solace would seep into her mind, a subliminal message to train her brain to feel at ease. I was convinced that it was the small moments in each day that would teach her there was a future, not too far away, when she would feel something other than sorrow.

There was still a long way to go, but her parents hadn't totally obliterated her spirit. I felt suddenly so proud of her. And seeing her small face breaking into a faint smile as she presented me with her second bookmark, even though it didn't quite yet reach her eyes, gave me the confidence that with our support she would get there.

Chapter 31

Salvation comes in unexpected ways and it was only as Phoebe began to lose her fear of leaving my side that I fully appreciated that hope had arrived. It turned out that she was an entrepreneur in the making, branching out from bookmarks to produce a whole range of products, including birthday cards and beaded bracelets made from macramé.

On the day of the much anticipated car boot sale I felt a warm-blooded, buoyant feeling in my stomach. Besides her excitement for the sale I sensed a re-emerging interest in the world around Phoebe was a sure sign of her recovery. Her appetite had increased and for a few weeks I had only cooked porridge on a couple of occasions, something I was thrilled about since the sight of the stuff sparked vivid memories of her retching and made me physically ill.

We pulled our overloaded car into the site of the sale at 6.30am. It was a windy day and as we tried to set up, the signs that Emily and Phoebe had so carefully prepared kept blowing over so that they were unreadable. Worried no one would show any interest in Phoebe's wares I had invited as many friends and neighbours as I could and, loyally, many of them turned up, each of them making a small purchase.

At first Phoebe hovered behind Emily, Jamie and me, refusing to involve herself, but as the morning went on she seemed to come to life – excited, I think, to see the things she had produced were in demand. Her eyes lost their weepy look and I completely lost any guilt I felt in setting her up.

With over half of her stock sold she gained the confidence to take the front line, even taking the money herself and counting out the change carefully, her lips moving as she worked out the amounts. It might not sound like that much of a big deal but it was a seismic step forwards as far as I was concerned.

It was as big a surprise to me as to her then to find that many other customers were showing an interest, actual strangers I'd never met before. I wasn't sure whether they were kindly passers-by who could tell that what we were selling was the work of a child, or if they genuinely liked what they saw, but many of them bought something.

As the crowds dispersed and just a few stragglers remained our table was virtually empty. While I took down the larger signs and balloons then folded up the paste table, Emily and Jamie, excited by the sight of the full money tin, were trying to convince Phoebe to let them buy into her business. Their enthusiasm soaked into her so that, not only was there a change in her energy, but also her colour. She looked as if someone had taken a brush and painted some pink on her cheeks.

Later that evening Phoebe arranged herself between Emily and me on the sofa, lying on her stomach with her elbows down and chin resting in her hands. We were halfway through watching an American sitcom when Jamie got up and went into the kitchen, rummaging through the cupboards for food, even though he'd only finished dinner an hour earlier.

'Pause it for me, Mum,' he said, as he swallowed down a Jaffa Cake and helped himself to another two.

Phoebe sat up. 'Can I have one of those?'

Jamie came back into the living room with the packet. 'Knock yourself out,' he said, still chomping. It was the first time since her disclosure that she had voluntarily reached for food and as she took a delicate nibble, I could have cried with relief.

Chapter 32

The first few weeks of the summer holiday passed, if not without a hitch, then certainly a lot more peacefully than the Easter break had. Phoebe's tantrums were becoming increasingly rare now and their cause easily identifiable. She still had a tendency to fly off the handle if plans were altered to any great extent, but I had learnt to give her plenty of warning if something arose in the day that wasn't already on our schedule and her reaction now seemed more panic-stricken than angry.

I certainly noticed that I was holding less tension myself. Painkillers for stress headaches were no longer obligatory at the end of my day and I no longer felt compelled to force an overly cheerful tone to compensate for Phoebe's dark moods, something that had been incredibly draining.

Almost every week we took a trip to the seaside. Phoebe adored playing cricket or frisbee on the beach and the exercise, coupled with nice weather, had brushed her skin with a soft glow so that she looked robust and healthy, almost unrecognisable from the girl who had arrived on my doorstep nearly five months earlier. Towards the end of July we met up with Jenny, Liz, Rachel and all of their children, so that our group totalled about 17. I was worried that Phoebe might be overwhelmed by the presence of lots of other children and at first she had held back, glued to my side while the rest of them played.

After a while Jamie tempted her into throwing pebbles in the sea and she joined him eagerly. Unfortunately, after only a couple of minutes the sea breeze, boisterous, threw one of Jamie's attempts off course and the pebble caught Phoebe on the top of her head. Like most children I have cared for, Phoebe possessed resilience that others lacked. She didn't cry, and apart from cradling the injured spot with a cupped hand, she made no fuss at all. I supposed that, having survived the degradation of repeated abuse, absorbing the impact of a small pebble was almost inconsequential. She bore the assault stoically but returned to my side, even more reluctant to join in than when she had first arrived.

I was hugely relieved when one of Rachel's charges, a girl slightly younger than Phoebe, approached and invited her to help build a sandcastle. Phoebe looked embarrassed and for a moment I thought she might refuse, but Laura smiled, leaned over, grabbed Phoebe's hand and pulled her to her feet. They both laughed and ran off, chasing each other to the group of children already at work with buckets and spades. I could have kissed Laura, and Rachel as well, who stood nearby, smiling. I guessed she'd put Laura up to it but it didn't matter – all of the other children had shifted around to make space for Phoebe, welcoming her into the fold.

I felt myself welling up but couldn't help smiling through tears at the sight of Phoebe as she stared around the circle of children. She certainly did more studying of them than digging – truly amazed, I think, to finally feel part of a group. When one of the children, a boy of about six, grew bored and wandered off towards the rock pool the others gradually followed. Soon only Phoebe was left beside their half-finished creation, a crestfallen expression on her face.

Three-year-old Billy, whom Phoebe had met before at Jenny's house, toddled back and yelled, 'Come on, FeeFee!' In seconds she was on her feet, running along beside him to join the others and leaving a flurry of sand in her wake.

When the children returned from the rock pool with a mangy-looking crab and armfuls of shells we cleaned them up, then ate lunch sitting on rugs on the sand, our backs leaning against the sea wall. Everyone had packed a picnic but we also bought chips from the beach-front shop, hot pasties and warm sugared doughnuts. Jamie was sprawled at my feet, reclined like a Roman emperor, his plate piled high. He feasted hungrily while Phoebe looked on, gazing at him with admiration.

After a few minutes Phoebe tucked in alongside everyone else, copying the other children by adding a bit of everything to her paper plate. It was a joy to watch her enjoying her food and I could hardly believe it when, 10 minutes later, she dived in for seconds.

After we'd eaten, Jenny trudged through the sand with a tray of teas and coffees and came over to share our rug. Billy, never far behind, sat on her lap as soon as her arms were free. With the sun shining, I couldn't have imagined a nicer place in the world to be than on a beach in the north of England. Closing my eyes, I could hear the delicate chink of pebbles as waves lapped the shore. The gentle breeze carried a salty tang and the peppery sweet perfume of seaweed. I inhaled deeply and stretched out my legs, relishing the warmth of the sun on my skin. It was the most relaxed I'd felt for a long time, I realised.

Gratefully sipping the scalding tea, I was about to ask whether Jenny, as that week's on-call foster carer, had had any emergency calls so far, when Phoebe interrupted: 'Jenny, did you know? When I came to the seaside with Daddy before he did horrible things to me with his willy.'

Jenny was startled, her eyes widening, though she quickly recovered. I could see that Liz and Rachel had also overheard by the way they suddenly sprang into action, trying to distract their charges.

'Honey, do you remember what I said? You can talk to me about that, but not when we're in public, OK?'

'*There's a time and a place, Phoebe, and this isn't it.*' She still used her combative tone to mock things I'd previously said to her but nowadays it was by way of a gentle teasing rather than a nasty sneer. Her ability to recognise the humour in it and to laugh at the way she used to be reconfirmed my conviction that most of her early symptoms were an invention of her own mind, a defence mechanism designed to push away anyone who might pose a threat to her.

The moment was soon forgotten when Laura grabbed Phoebe's hand again. 'Come on, we're going to hunt for flat pebbles and shells.' Rachel had mentioned that she sometimes found Laura's controlling ways exasperating but there were times when a foster child's dominance came in useful and Phoebe seemed happy to fall in with her new friend's plans. I think she was so bowled over to have someone keen on playing with her that she would have gone along with it, even if it happened to be something she didn't want to do.

Later, the girls held hands and paddled at the water's edge. The sea breeze caught the hems of their dresses and the light material fluttered like the wings of the gulls swooping above them. It was funny to think that anyone watching from the promenade would have got the impression that Phoebe, out for the day with her loving family, hadn't a care in the world.

The children were taken by surprise when a rogue wave crested in, spraying their clothes and making them shiver with cold. Shrieking, Phoebe turned around and searched the beach for me. Jenny had been aiming her camera at the pair and happened to capture the image just as Phoebe locked eyes with mine: her face, framed by ripples of damp, dark golden hair, was a picture of shocked delight.

I still have the photo, displayed on the living-room wall. Remembering the depth of her misery when she acknowledged what her parents had done, I found her animated expression that day a stark reminder of the staggering progress she had made in a short space of time. Now, whenever I look at the way the laughter reaches her eyes, it reminds me how proud I felt to see her so happy.

It's the way I love to remember her.

Towards the end of August, feeling confident that the trip wouldn't prove too unsettling for Phoebe, we rented a cottage in the Lake District. Phoebe seemed tense during the journey, even regressing by mimicking everything we said. Emily, Jamie and me exchanged glances, all wondering whether a week in the confines of a small cottage was such a good idea after all.

It was a relief to get out of the car and as Phoebe rushed into our holiday home I hung back to reassure my gloomy children that we didn't have to stay the whole week, if Phoebe had reverted to her old ways. At least the cottage had been a good choice, full of old-fashioned charm, with an inglenook fireplace, floral sofas and oak-beamed, low ceilings.

A loud clattering upstairs drew my attention away from a tour of the picturesque garden. My heart sank as I ran up the stairs, wondering what damage Phoebe might have inflicted, but it seemed the noise arose from her running from room to room, opening cupboards, wardrobes and doors and looking under beds.

'What are you doing, Phoebe?'

'*What are you doing, Phoebe?*'

Tired after our long journey, I snapped at her. 'Get downstairs and help us with the cases, please.'

By dinnertime she had relaxed and the mimicking, thankfully, stopped. I knew that she had found holidays traumatic in the past, and then it occurred to me that she was probably conducting a sweep of the place when she first arrived, perhaps frightened that her father would once again join her in the bedroom of her holiday home.

Phoebe, Emily and Jamie were all seated at the large dining table when I served our dinner but as I set the plates of Spaghetti Bolognaise in front of them, Phoebe began to retch loudly.

'Oh no, not *that* again!' Jamie, ravenous after our journey, looked at Phoebe in disgust. 'Mum, tell her to stop.'

But Phoebe waggled her index finger in the air. 'Ha ha, gotcha!' Then she threw her head back and bellowed and we all joined in, amazed by her ability to laugh at herself. She thought it was a great joke and smiled away to herself as she tucked into her dinner. I got the sense that this fun-loving, gentle girl was the real Phoebe, finally taking tentative steps to freedom after being trapped for so long. The rest of the week passed without incident and was so enjoyable that I began to marvel again that I was able to earn a living in such an amazing way.

It was a shock then, just after 4am one Friday morning at the beginning of September, to hear footsteps on the stairs. As I sat bolt upright and reached for my dressing gown, my heart strummed against my chest. Instinct had told me that

Phoebe, though still sometimes volatile, was no longer a risk to herself and so I had gotten out of the habit of cat-napping with one ear tuned for trouble. I flew down the stairs to see what was wrong and was confronted in the living room by Phoebe, bright-eyed and already dressed. She greeted me with a warm smile. Even in my tired state it occurred to me that she no longer woke looking tired, freed from the terrors that had stalked her nights for such a long time.

'Shall I make breakfast today?' she asked, all trace of monotone gone.

Startled by her spirited voice, I had no choice but to agree. 'But not yet, honey. It's barely morning – much too early to be up.'

Thankfully she went back to bed and so did I, but I was awoken a couple of hours later by the sound of clattering saucepans.

'Can we make pancakes now, Rosie?' she asked, reaching into the cupboard with unexpected agility. She was so insistent on making the mixture herself that I left her to it. She'd gone so many days without a tantrum that I didn't want to set one off and only joined in when it was time for frying. I did my best to bang out all the lumps with the spatula, but there was only so much I could do and the result left a lot to be desired.

Phoebe insisted that the first pancake was for Jamie, who had just got up, drawn by the smell of cooking.

Jamie took the plate, eyeing the contents dubiously, then gave me a queasy-looking glance. I resolutely ignored it, reaching for a plate and serving some for myself.

'Is it nice?' she asked, her eyes alight.

I took a tentative bite: it was revoltingly eggy.

'Lovely,' I said.

She smiled, turning to Jamie. Dutifully he had a nibble before giving me a 'What in the Hell is this?' expression. I returned a hard, meaningful stare and thankfully he managed, 'Mmm, nice.'

Chapter 33

Phoebe had made such rapid progress through the summer holidays that by the time the new term arrived in September 2009 it was clear to me that she was in the wrong school. Annoyed that I hadn't got the wheels in motion sooner, once I had dropped her off to her Year 5 classroom (trembling from top to toe, with tears streaming down her cheeks), I was determined to get to work finding a mainstream school that could deal with her needs.

Cognitively, for the most part, she was no different to any other child. Throughout the holiday I had worked through some exercise books with her, and, as far as I could tell, educationally she had caught up to the point where she wouldn't stand out from other children her age. Behaviourally, I knew that she might prove a bit of a challenge – at home with me she was fine, but she still tended to kick off when surrounded by large groups and was prone to outbursts of inappropriate comments – but compared to when we had first met she was far calmer and I was sure that our local primary schools had encountered worse.

First off, I tried Lenke. The local authority would have the most sway in persuading a school to accept a new child, but as expected I was met with a loud sigh and general lethargy: if Phoebe already had a school place, what was the point in moving her? But the social worker had no major objection to the move, providing I did all of the legwork myself.

It took the rest of the day to pinpoint two possibilities, one being a primary less than half a mile from our house. When I explained our situation to the secretary of Glenhaven Primary School, I felt a slight shiver, the sort of feeling that comes when you can sense something positive is about to happen. As soon as I mentioned the word 'foster' there was a slight pause and then a change of tone, from brisk and efficient to empathetic.

The head teacher sounded equally understanding and also, I sensed, a little intrigued when I gave him an idea of Phoebe's history. He agreed to a meeting the next day to discuss it further. I wasn't sure how Phoebe would take the news that another change might be imminent. However much she disliked school, she had attended Englebrook since she was nursery age and it was familiar.

I was going to put off broaching the subject until the morning but when I picked her up from school she looked so lost and alone as she waited with the other children to be dismissed that I went for it there and then. Slipping my arm around her shoulder as we walked to the car, I said,

'How would you like to come with me and have a look around a different school tomorrow?'

'A different one?' she eyed me suspiciously and I tensed, hoping I hadn't triggered a tantrum outside the school gates. It would be difficult to get her to the car if that was the case.

'Yes, one much nearer to our house – we wouldn't have to drive in the mornings, we could walk.'

'Cool,' she said casually, adopting one of Jamie's much-used replies. It was as simple as that. We went home and nothing more was mentioned about it for the rest of the day.

In the morning I had time to give Emily and Jamie lifts to school since our appointment with the head teacher of Glenhaven Primary School wasn't until 9.30am. Before we even entered the playground I felt a level of confidence in the school that had been missing at Englebrook. Impressively, following my initial enquiry about a possible place for Phoebe, the head teacher, a Mr Sands, had called me back later that day. He wanted more details about Phoebe's past but was thoughtful enough to know it would be demeaning if discussed in front of her, so he had cleared half an hour from his schedule to run through what he needed to know.

When I met Mr Sands in person I felt even more reassured. His handshake was firm – always a good start in my book – and Phoebe seemed to sense a natural warmth within him, smiling instead of her usual reaction to strangers of curling her lip in a sneer.

'I think,' Mr Sands said, leaning forward and forming a pyramid with his fingers, 'what might be a good idea is for Phoebe to spend a morning with us, to see if we're the right place for her and vice-versa. Would you like that, Phoebe?'

That morning I had already coached her on appropriate replies if the head teacher directed any questions her way. I warned her not to mention anything private, meaning anything to do with her parents, and she was strictly forbidden from repeating anything he said, but my lecture wouldn't necessarily hold much weight, depending on what mood she was in. I found myself clenching my knees tightly together, praying she would cooperate.

She glanced at me and smiled before opening her mouth. 'Yes, please.'

I let out a breath of relief before masking it with a slight cough. Phoebe smirked. She was enjoying herself, the little rascal.

'Excellent. How about today then, since you've got the day off?'

My eyes widened and I turned to gauge her reaction. I hadn't anticipated the offer and wasn't too sure it was a good idea. I would have preferred to do some more coaching before letting her loose on the staff, but it seemed I was out of luck – Phoebe was nodding with enthusiasm and Mr Sands had already pushed back his chair, offering me his hand once again and telling me to return after lunch at 1pm to collect her.

* * *

I couldn't settle at home and set about clearing up the house like a whirling dervish. The direst scenarios kept rushing through my mind – flying crockery and loud retching in the school canteen, teachers being mimicked or kicked, children mocked or sworn at. It was behaviour I hadn't seen at home from Phoebe in quite a while but in the company of strangers she did tend to revert to her old, defensive ways. It can take a while for children to learn that boundaries move with them.

As I vacuumed, part of me regretted not being more honest with Mr Sands in our telephone conversation. I had told him that the level of abuse she had experienced was severe and that her mental health had suffered as a result but I hadn't been specific, knowing that it was unlikely she'd be given the chance of a place at a mainstream school if I was entirely honest. Having cursed a stream of social workers in the past for withholding information, there I was, doing exactly the same thing.

It was an eye-opener, to be truthful, and suddenly I could understand why an over-worked social worker, perhaps with a child sat beside their desk at 5pm on a Friday evening, might stretch the truth in order to get that child a safe, warm bed for the night. I had a horrible feeling that my good intentions might bite back at me and as I left the house I convinced myself that shielding the whole truth might have been wholly irresponsible.

As it turned out, I needn't have worried. When I returned to Glenhaven I was delighted to find Phoebe, flushed with excitement, refusing to leave and come home with me.

'Please, Rosie, they've got Art this afternoon. Can I stay, please?'

Mr Sands smiled and held up his hands in surrender.

'It's up to you, Mrs Lewis. Phoebe's had a wonderful morning so we'd be happy to accept her straight away, if you'd both like?'

Phoebe was nodding vigorously. I laughed. 'I can't argue with that, can I?'

After switching schools, Phoebe went from strength to strength. The staff really seemed to 'get' her. Often I was approached as I waited in the playground at the end of the school day by a teacher who wanted to tell me some funny anecdote about something Phoebe had said or done; even the children welcomed her. I think they found her a little eccentric, but mercifully she was all the more popular because of it. Her thirst for knowledge meant she got along well with the teaching staff and apparently the rest of the class fed on her enthusiasm.

At the end of the day she sometimes left me waiting at the school gates while she hung back, chatting with friends, and I couldn't have been happier to be abandoned. Our walk home would be filled with chatter as she updated me on what she'd learnt and bits about the other children.

She seemed to be fascinated by one boy in particular – Joshua, who sat at the same group table as her. He always seemed to be in trouble for something, whether it was throwing missiles in class (an act Phoebe, ironically, seemed outraged by) or swearing at the teacher. One day she came out of school looking glum and told me that Joshua had pulled her plaits so hard during one of the lessons that it had made her eyes water. She said that he'd then kicked the girl who sat opposite under the desk, scribbled over her maths homework and told the teacher to 'fuck off'. It was a shame this Joshua character was in her class, I thought, making up my mind to ask if Phoebe could be moved to another group. With all that she'd been through, it was best if she could be steered away from someone so volatile. 'What about the other boys? Are they alright? Who is your favourite of all the boys?'

She rolled her eyes at me. 'Joshua, of course,' she said, as if the answer was entirely obvious. I laughed, but actually the implications weren't at all funny: I had an inkling that when she was older, Phoebe would be in danger of being attracted to the Joshuas of this world, as women who had been abused as little girls often were.

Apart from regular updates on Joshua's antics, everything else she mentioned about Glenhaven was positive and thankfully there was no sign of school phobia. Phoebe was usually the first up and ready in her school uniform while the rest of us sloped around in our dressing gowns.

There were still times when she sat motionless, a stricken look on her face, and I knew that sad memories were running through her mind. One day after school, instead of skipping from the playground to meet me she trudged wearily along and remained silent for the whole journey home.

For the next hour she hovered by my side but brushed off all of my attempts to get her talking. It was when I invited her to help peel the potatoes for dinner that she first spoke. I think the repetitive action gave her something to focus on, allowing the jumble of thoughts in her head to form themselves linearly enough for her to put a voice to them.

'Robin and Phillipa didn't ever really love me, did they, Rosie? Not like you do.'

I stopped peeling and stood with the knife poised in mid-air, momentarily disorientated by the sudden use of her parents' first names. Until then she had always referred to them as Mummy and Daddy. So, that's how she's going to cope with acknowledging such an ugly truth, I thought, by distancing herself from them.

It was difficult to know how to respond. Whatever the Steadmans had done, they were still her parents. I wasn't sure what agreeing with her would do to her self-esteem. 'Well,' I answered slowly, 'I actually think that all parents love their children, Phoebe. It's just that love doesn't always stop them behaving very badly.'

She hid her face from me so I couldn't see her expression but she nodded, seemingly satisfied. Once Jamie and Emily joined us at the dinner table Phoebe had rallied and began to join in with their noisy banter. After that, she rarely mentioned her mother or her father.

* * *

By the October half-term our family had completely recovered its equilibrium and Phoebe was 'one of us'. The days were still pleasantly warm and the week away from school passed quickly with all our day trips; it was so harmonious that we even dared an overnight stay in London. Phoebe fell quiet as our train neared the city and the anguished look on her face told me she was thinking of her father. I squeezed her hand and our eyes locked for several moments.

'I used to come here with Daddy, Rosie.'

'I know, sweetie. I know.'

Had it been possible at that moment, I would have reached in and extracted all the hurt from her mind, even if it meant absorbing it into my own. But then I realised that by seeking comfort when bad memories overwhelmed her, Phoebe was learning to overwrite the pain by herself. Sure enough, after drawing strength from a quick hug, she lifted her head and drifted across the aisle to Jamie. He nudged her playfully with his shoulder when she sat beside him and soon they were pointing out some of the famous London landmarks, consigning her parents to where they belonged, folded away in a distant corner of the past.

The mild weather faltered with the beginning of the new school term and one particularly crisp day, when Phoebe had been living with us for nearly eight months, Des phoned with some unwelcome news.

'Phoebe's to be moved, Rosie, I'm afraid.'

My heart plummeted. A knot tightened itself in my

stomach and climbed quickly to my throat so that my voice, when I eventually found it, sounded strained.

'Moving? Why?'

'The local authority has a carer with an unexpected vacancy and she's willing to accept long-termers.'

'Willing to accept?' I responded acidly. It was as if Phoebe were faulty goods and lucky to be given a home.

'I know, Rosie. I know how you feel and I'm sure it wasn't meant in that way. And I'm not just saying this but she does sound ideal for Phoebe. Apparently she heard about Phoebe's startling progress and she's fascinated, so it seems. She's a social worker with experience of special needs.'

'Ah, so now it comes out,' I said, shocking myself with an irrepressible sneer. I was livid. 'Not only saving money but looking after one of their own into the bargain.' Even though as an agency carer I receive similar allowances to my local authority counterparts, agencies, running as private businesses, charge a fee on top of this. If social services manage to identify one of their own carers with a vacancy, it is cheaper for them to cover the cost of their own carer's allowances than find the money for agency fees. I could understand that budgets were tightly stretched and that they had to look for savings where possible, but to me uprooting a happy child for the sake of saving money seemed fundamentally wrong.

'Rosie …' Des said chidingly, sending me the message that I was in danger of becoming unreasonable.

'Sorry, Des, but she's just got settled in her new school and she loves it.' The timing couldn't have been worse, as far as I was concerned. Sadly, it wasn't unusual for children to be moved for financial reasons.

'You know how it works, Rosie. And once you've calmed down you might see that Phoebe is more than ready for a move.'

'What child is ever ready for a move?' I retorted. 'She's happy, Des. Perhaps for the first time ever. Why can't they just leave her be?'

Sudden endings are not unusual with fostering so I should have been primed and ready for this unexpected change of plans, but I found my thoughts were reeling as I tried to catch up with reality. Despite the shifting sands of her existence, Phoebe had managed to root herself in our family and was finally blossoming into the girl she should have been allowed to be years earlier. It seemed so unfair to uproot her just when she was beginning to triumph.

'You're right, she is happy. And that tells me that your work with her is done.'

But I didn't reply. I couldn't – there were tears rolling down my cheeks.

Des let out a breath. When he spoke it was with affectionate exasperation.

'Rosie, my love, when are you going to learn? Fostering is not meant to last forever – there always comes a time when you have to let go.'

Chapter 34

The arrival of November brought a sharper edge to the weather. Early morning frosts were taking longer to recede and the evening chill began anchoring itself from mid-afternoon so that we'd arrive home after the school run with pinched faces and icy feet. Phoebe seemed to feel the cold more intensely than the rest of us and for her the garden lost its appeal. She no longer asked to go out and play with Jamie, who happily tore along the frozen path on his skateboard, oblivious to the icy wind despite wearing only a thin T-shirt and jeans.

Already the lawn was covered with a blanket of red and brown leaves and the forget-me-nots that had bloomed so gloriously just weeks earlier sagged close to the icy earth in sad, dying twists. And with the lowered winter sun came another change, one that Phoebe welcomed with as much enthusiasm as the blustery weather.

Trapped

Despite having my hands full with Emily's fifteenth birthday and Christmas looming, a particularly persuasive social worker from the local authority had signed me up as the out-of-hours foster carer for the area. Three-year-old Charlie was the result, arriving in the early hours on a freezing cold night in the middle of the month, accompanied by a police officer and a duty social worker. The traumatised boy had spent most of the evening in Casualty after falling from a balcony and breaking his arm. His mother, drunk to the point of semi-consciousness, lay totally unaware of his distress in their first-floor flat.

The morning after his arrival he awoke crying, bewildered to find himself in an unfamiliar bed. My own children were, as usual, delighted with the new addition but Phoebe kept her distance as I introduced everyone, not quite so pleased to find an interloper in her midst. As Emily and Jamie fussed around him, she eyed the toddler with suspicion and hung back as we gave him a tour of the house. Charlie barely left my side during his first day with us and Phoebe was unusually clingy too, shadowing me everywhere I went. I gave her lots of cuddles but it seemed wrong to reassure her that her position in our family was safe, when I knew that it was far from it.

Two weeks later when Charlie moved on to one of the local authority's own carers, Phoebe was bereft. She had grown fond of having someone younger around and surprised me with the tenderness she had shown him. I think his sudden departure reminded her of the loss she had already experienced, as well as accentuating the insecurity of her own position.

Saying goodbye to Charlie was like having an echo from the past catch up with me. Watching the effect his departure had on Phoebe reminded me of the difficult times when it had been particularly painful for me to say goodbye. The ability to let go was crucial in a foster carer and I had managed it many times before, but it was a criterion in the 'job spec' that I still struggled with and the strain of working through the sadness took its toll. As well as the prospect of losing Phoebe I had to admit I was dreading the actual handover.

To give the child time to adjust to the idea of moving families, social services plan a transition period of around six weeks, starting with a short meeting at the foster carer's house on the first day, say, a two-hour visit to have a chat and a cup of tea. The new carers then gradually integrate themselves into the child's life: collecting them from school, taking them out on trips and progressing to sleepovers. The ultimate goal is that the child spends more time at their new carer's house until finally the handover is complete. During this period, the foster carer is supposed to withdraw emotionally, while being present physically, so that the child understands that approval is given for them to transfer their attachment.

Besides finding the severing of close ties a brutal process, being in the company of strangers for such a long, drawn-out period of time is in itself a draining experience and so as the handover period neared it felt as if a dark cloud was hovering above my head. In some ways, even though I didn't want to lose Phoebe, part of me wanted the whole process over with quickly, but the permanency team had decided it would be best not to unsettle her with talk of moving until after Christmas.

The festive season was often a difficult time for children in care, particularly the first one away from their parents, and they didn't want to add to Phoebe's stress. As it was, she coped with all the celebrations brilliantly and seemed genuinely excited, particularly as she used the money she had raised from the sale of her bookmarks to buy each of us an individual surprise present. She had enlisted the help of one of her teachers to make the purchases, something she was incredibly proud of.

'And there's nothing we can do to keep her, I'm afraid,' I told Jamie as we sat side by side on the sofa, the night after New Year's Day. I was due to meet Maxine, Phoebe's new foster carer, later that week and decided I couldn't put off telling Jamie and Emily any longer. The news had hit my son hard and he reacted angrily, gutted the one member of the family who could always be relied upon to be wicket keeper, backstop or whatever other role he had in mind was being taken from us. Not only that, but I think, like the rest of us, he felt protective towards Phoebe.

'What if we leave Bright Heights and register with the local authority? It won't cost them any extra for Phoebe to stay where she is then, will it?'

Resigning from our agency and transferring to the local authority was something I had considered, but quickly dismissed.

'We'd have to face a panel at Bright Heights to be released and it would take at least six months to transfer to the local authority. They'd need to do all the checks and interviews again. The bean counters want to start saving money immediately, Jamie – they wouldn't allow it.'

His eyes filled with tears and he swiped at them with the back of his hand.

'So we won't ever see her again?'

'Of course we will,' I said, swallowing an anxious sigh. I could hear how unsure I sounded. As I reached an arm out to hug him, my heart lurched. 'Don't be upset. She'll be going into long-term care, to a place where she can spend the rest of her childhood. That's a good thing.'

'But she could have stayed here forever,' Jamie insisted gloomily. He shrugged me off and said good night, going off to bed voluntarily for the first time in 11 years. Sighing again, I switched on the TV and tried to find a channel that would absorb me enough to still the swirling guilt I felt at exposing my children to another painful ending.

But it wasn't just Jamie's reaction that had churned my emotions – I still had to break the news to Phoebe. Like police officers, foster carers have to accept that imparting bad news comes with the territory. Whether it's telling a child that their parent hasn't made the effort to turn up for contact or that a judge has decided they must spend the rest of their childhood in foster care, being the bearer of bad news is never easy and I wasn't at all sure how Phoebe would take it.

Going into long-term care is a daunting experience for vulnerable children and, besides the upheaval of moving house and perhaps area, they must also cope with the trauma of saying goodbye to their foster family too. Children who are already struggling to cope with a sense of loss are sometimes left with a lifelong feeling of being unlovable. It's human nature to want to belong and rejection is difficult for anyone to deal with, let alone a child like Phoebe. Adults who have been made redundant sometimes struggle to come to terms with their feelings. I couldn't help stewing over how much more devastating it must be for a child with Phoebe's experiences. Giving up on the TV, I tried to read a book but the words shimmered on the page in front of me. There was nothing I could do to soothe my anxiety.

So the next day, as soon as I set eyes on Maxine, I felt my whole body sag with relief. Des had accompanied me to the local authority offices and as we made our way up to the canteen on the second floor I was glad of his company, not only for the moral support (I always seem to imagine the worst when meeting long-term carers) but also his gregarious nature. Des was the sort of person who roused people into banter, wherever he might be – at a bus stop, supermarket or dentist's waiting room. I knew he could be relied upon to recharge any lapse in conversation.

The social worker, who must have noticed our lingering stares as we entered the café, pushed her chair back and smiled broadly. Dressed casually in jeans and a long-sleeved top, she walked over to greet us with her hand extended.

An attractive woman in her early 40s, she wore her dark hair pulled back from her face and piled up into a wide clip at the top of her head so that her eyes, bright blue and intelligent, sparkled as she smiled. The small wire-framed glasses she wore suited her delicate features and I realised with a jolt that she actually looked like an older version of Phoebe. When she shook my hand it was with vigour, a full-bodied, friendly greeting.

We spent the next hour chatting about Phoebe and the journey she had made so far. I found myself with so much to say that Des barely got a look in: Maxine was fascinated by the Applied Behavioural Analysis and in turn I was comforted to find that she truly seemed to want to continue working through the programme with Phoebe. The social worker came across as solid, resourceful and above all, she had a wicked sense of humour, something she might need to rely on in the first few weeks while Phoebe settled.

So when I picked Phoebe up from school later in the week I wasn't feeling quite as anxious as I might have been about breaking the news to her that she was going to move. Sitting side by side on the sofa that evening, I flicked the TV to mute and told her that Lenke had been in touch with some news.

A flicker of sadness crossed her face before I said any more and I realised she was expecting news of her parents. 'It's alright, there's nothing to worry about,' I told her. Of course it was a daft thing to say, knowing that it was highly likely that the news *would* cause her to worry. 'Lenke has been in touch with a lady who would love to meet you. She has a lovely house and no children of her own …'

Her eyes widened in alarm and so I hesitated, feeling a lump form in my throat. Giving a child news knowing it will cause them pain was really one of the most awful aspects of fostering and I detested doing it. 'She'd really like you to go and stay with her.'

A spread of colour appeared on her cheeks. Her feelings were evident from the pain on her face but quickly she tried to cover it, twisting her expression into an ugly sneer. Reverting to her old behaviour, she stuck her index fingers in her ears and mimicked me, '*She'd like you to go and stay with her.*' And then after that, every time I tried to talk to her she screeched, 'la, la, la,' her fingers still rammed in her ears, although she wasn't so accomplished at retreating behind a wall of bizarre behaviour as she had once been – her voice wobbled and then a twin track of tears appeared on her cheeks.

The painful resentment in her eyes stabbed at my heart and I felt treacherous. How cruel life can be, I thought, not for the first time feeling a childlike rage at the unfairness of it all.

As the first day of introductions approached Phoebe regressed, her arm flapping and spinning returning with a vengeance. She also fired insults at me under her breath, telling me how much she hated me, how she longed to leave. I knew it was an attempt to sever our bond in a way that would cause her the least distress but the fact that she was hurting broke my heart and although I didn't want her to leave, I longed for the pain of the move to be over, for everyone's sake. It had been so long since she'd behaved in that way and it was such a bizarre sight that we all couldn't help but gawp at her. Her nerves, expressed so physically, became contagious and so the night before Maxine was due to visit, I felt nauseous with anxiety.

When I woke Phoebe the next morning she seemed terrified and I couldn't blame her. She barely touched her breakfast and when I tried to encourage her, she barked loudly at me. The doorbell rang and I wondered how Maxine would react when she saw her new charge staggering behind me with a bizarre gait and howling like a wolf.

I should have had more faith in her. Maxine breezed in and pulled me into a friendly hug. We had arranged to welcome each other with the enthusiasm of long-lost relatives, knowing children find it easier to move on if the person they feel loyal to approves of their new carer. Phoebe hung around behind me, rumpling up the fabric of my blouse with fidgety fingers. Intrigued by all our affectionate greetings, she dared a peep around my shoulder, ducking back again when Maxine smiled and said hello.

As I prepared refreshments for everyone Phoebe remained glued to my side. The ritual of lining up the cups and boiling the kettle didn't dispel the nervous flutter in my stomach although I was grateful that, for now, Phoebe had stopped barking. As I stirred the drinks, I noticed my hands trembling, the hot liquid spilling over onto the worktop.

Phoebe looked even more anxious than I felt, overwhelmed by Maxine's attempts to engage her in conversation, but there were two pink spots on her cheeks and her eyes were shining. She looked prettier than I'd ever seen her before.

The social worker seemed to take Phoebe's mimicking in her stride, continuing to chat with me and trying to include her as much as she could, although on the way out Maxine asked if she could have a quiet word. I put the door on the latch and we walked out onto the driveway. Maxine cupped her hand under my elbow and leaned in to ask under her breath, 'How often does she, you know, repeat what you say?'

I could sense her apprehension and for a fleeting moment I was tempted to say, 'Every time anyone opens their mouth.' I remembered how Phoebe's mimicking had really got under my skin in the early days after her arrival, making me feel tense and irritable and, unfairly, I was hoping that Maxine might flee and leave our happy family unit undisturbed. Forcing myself to put my own selfish agenda aside, I hesitated then answered honestly, 'She hasn't parroted us for months, really – she's only doing it because she's nervous. As soon as she's settled, I'm sure she'll stop doing it. Oh, and the funny walk will vanish as well.'

Her shoulders slumped with relief and she thanked me profusely before climbing into her car.

* * *

A week later the introductions were progressing well. Maxine had visited several times and Phoebe was warming to her, so much so that she stopped parroting and was actively engaging in conversations, even volunteering information without being prompted. On the following Monday, Maxine collected her from school for the first time and when they got into the car, it was to her that Phoebe chattered about the day's events.

I fussed around offering them snacks and refilling their glasses but they took little notice of me, already forming their own tight-knit group. According to our handover plan, today was to be their first outing without me accompanying them. I suggested the local park and then back for dinner, but it seemed that they had already settled on going for a pizza.

Even though I had spent several nights praying that Phoebe would be happy in her new situation, witnessing it happening before my eyes felt jarring, so much so that I left the room for a few minutes, busying myself in the kitchen. I only returned once they were dressed in their coats, ready to embark on their trip. Maxine gave a little wave as she left but I was choked to see that Phoebe barely glanced backwards. Tormented by my sudden anonymity, I tried to rationalise my feelings, but I was still struggling when Des popped around later in the day.

'It's like the last nine months didn't happen – she's almost as distant as the first day she came.'

'And that's exactly as it should be. She's moving on, Rosie. She has no choice in that. Phoebe knows that she's losing you and she's letting you go in the way that's going to hurt the least.'

'I know, I know that. It's just that …' How could I put into words that Phoebe moving on reconfirmed my own dispensability? Of course I knew that the day would come, but it had happened so abruptly that my emotions hadn't quite caught up. And with the arrival of someone new in Phoebe's life I felt more protective of her than ever, just as I was going to have to relinquish her. As usual, it was as if Des could hear my internal musings.

'She'll always remember you – you know that, don't you? What you've done for her won't just disappear because she's leaving.'

Still rankled, I answered with a sniff. Des smiled and took me by surprise, drawing me into an unexpected hug. I laid my head on his chest and for a moment I allowed myself to relax into him, aware that he had begun to stroke my hair. Feeling the tears forming, I abruptly pulled away, repressing my longing for someone kind and capable to take control. Briskly I assured him that I was fine.

'Rosie,' he said softly, his voice slightly hoarse. He shook his head as he walked down the path and I felt, not for the first time, that I had disappointed him.

Alone in the house, I got to work on Phoebe's life story book. In the past, when children came into the care system, foster carers often didn't think to keep the mementos that a loving parent would – cinema tickets, photos, cherished cuddly toys etc. And so care leavers often had nothing tangible from childhood to remind them of special people and memorable moments in their life. Nowadays foster carers are taught the importance of keeping memories safe and encouraged to keep a full record of the time they spent together.

Besides filling a memory box for Phoebe, I prepared one for Emily and Jamie, so that they would have a physical reminder of their time with her. As well as a photograph album, my own children's box contained items that I couldn't possibly have put in Phoebe's: the empty bubble bath bottle she drank from and alarmed us all into thinking she was poisoned, a cut-out corner from a box of porridge and a take-away pizza delivery leaflet. I hoped to make them laugh but I wouldn't allow them to open it until Phoebe had moved on, through fear of offending her.

Phoebe was delivered back in time for dinner, rosy-cheeked and looking happy. She didn't volunteer much, even though I framed my questions in many different ways. I supposed that I had to get used to being an outsider; she was transferring her attachment and that entailed severing the one she shared with me. It was natural.

The night before the final handover we all sat on the sofa watching a comedy, even though none of us were in the mood to laugh. Phoebe was staring at the TV, but like the rest of us, she wasn't really watching. When I noticed that her lips were shiny with saliva and the tears on her face I leaned over and tried to draw her into a hug but she pushed me away. I was used to being rejected in the last few days of a placement – I think children sense that the way to survive the separation is to slowly withdraw, which is what Phoebe was doing. Even though I understood, it still hurt: she looked so sad and alone.

Later, she rested her head on my shoulder to say goodnight, holding it there for longer than she needed to.

Chapter 35

It was a bitterly cold day when I drove Phoebe to a village on the borders of Birmingham, the grey sky reflecting my own downcast mood. During the journey to Maxine's house I kept up a steady stream of jovial chatter, though it was a strain, and by the lack of response from Phoebe in the back of the car, I could tell my efforts were failing.

As we pulled into the drive I noticed a small movement of the curtains in one of the downstairs windows. When I turned in my seat and caught the look on Phoebe's face a ripple of pity twisted through me. She looked so young and full of angst.

'Will I ever see you again, Rosie?'

She asked it in a straightforward way but the question really stirred up my emotions again. I hadn't told her anything about the siblings I had cared for, so she had no idea of the poignancy of her question.

'Of course you will. I'll be Auntie Rosie and you can see me whenever you like.'

I hoped that would be the case. Having met Maxine, I was sure it would be.

Any further conversation was stopped by the opening of the front door. Maxine walked towards our car, smiling as Phoebe and I clambered out. The social worker reached out her arms. All Phoebe had to do was walk a few feet towards her and yet she hesitated, turning to fix her eyes on me. It was as if the distance between Phoebe and her new carer was a bridge and as she contemplated taking the steps towards her new life I couldn't help but think that the drawbridge would be drawn up after her, as it had been with Tess and Harry.

Phoebe's eyes darted between us and I wondered if a fear of being disloyal was holding her back.

'Go on, Phoebe. It's cold. Don't keep Maxine waiting,' I told her. It was a strain to keep the emotion out of my voice but somehow I managed to sound light-hearted. She gave me a nervous smile and I nodded reassuringly. And so she edged towards Maxine, tiptoeing as if this would be a safer way of embarking on this new adventure.

Suddenly she was by my side again, howling and clinging tightly to my coat. Turning her tear-streaked face to mine she said, 'I'll miss you, Rosie.' Her voice was hoarse with emotion.

'I'll miss you too, very much.' I kissed the top of her head, my own eyes now misted with tears.

Briskly she pulled away and went to Maxine, who was clearly moved herself. She dabbed her eyes on her sleeve and Phoebe turned to glance back at me. After giving me a small wave she allowed herself to be guided into the house. Maxine mouthed a 'thank you' and smiled warmly before she closed the door.

And so it was done. Another ending.

As I drove home I allowed all the anxiety I felt for Phoebe to wash over me. The tears flowed as I fretted about the adjustments she was going to have to make – the relocation to an unfamiliar area, strange house, new carer, change of school. After all she'd been through it seemed like too much for a young girl to have to cope with. And what if she regressed – would Maxine be able to manage her? I wondered. It wasn't always easy being a single carer, as I well knew.

Every time I slowed or stopped in traffic I wondered what the drivers in the other cars around me must think of the sobbing woman with wild blonde hair and a swollen face. Keeping my eyes on the road, I leaned over to the glove compartment and reached for the box of tissues I always kept in there, but it was almost empty, reminding me of the drive I took with Phoebe and the trust she had placed in me when she finally told me what her father had done. The memory brought a fresh wave of tears.

When I got home it felt eerily quiet, so much so that I was actually grateful when the telephone rang. I was surprised to hear Lenke's voice, calling to find out how the handover had gone.

'As well as we could have expected, I think, Lenke – she's a brave girl.'

There was a sigh, a pause, and then she surprised me even more by apologising for her initial reluctance to open the family up to close scrutiny – 'We don't always get it right. I'm sorry to say that I let the wool be pulled over my eyes. Thank goodness she trusted you enough to let us know what was really going on in that house. You did good, Rosie, very good.' There was a sincerity in her tone that brought warmth to my heart and before hanging up, I thanked her gratefully.

Any delay in getting help for Phoebe wasn't Lenke's fault, not really. Cruelty was bound to be harder to identify if veiled behind the surface gloss of money and prestige. It was likely, I thought, that all of us drifted past abuse of one kind or another as we went about our everyday lives. Manipulative abusers kept their secrets well hidden and sometimes outsiders were too distracted or perhaps wilfully blind, unable to see beyond the veneers that had been carefully constructed.

That night I dreamed that a sudden earthquake struck the north of England, our house crumbling with the force of its tremor. Desolately, I wandered through the ruins searching for faceless children and shouting their names, all the while knowing in my heart that there was no way of reaching them beneath the rubble. I clawed until my fingers grew bloody and still I didn't stop but the missing little ones had fallen beyond my reach.

I woke with a start, enveloped by a feeling of gloom. Thankfully an early text from Maxine proved to be immensely cheering. Apparently Phoebe had announced,

'Auntie Rosie makes much better pancakes.' Maxine said that Phoebe was looking forward to our visit and hoping I would bring some pancakes along with me. The contact reassured me that she was willing to stay in touch and the thought that, in some small way, I would remain a part of Phoebe's life, was enough to quell the anxiety I had for her.

One morning, not long after she left us, I went into her room for the first time since she'd gone, armed with a box of cleaning equipment and a pair of rubber gloves. Already I had received several calls about new placements but I knew I wasn't ready to replace Phoebe quite so soon.

Pulling open the curtains, I saw that Phoebe had taped a picture of a butterfly to the glass. She must have copied one of Emily's stick-arounds onto a piece of paper then coloured it and cut it out. I wondered whether she did it with the same scissors she had used to harm herself on that shocking day, many months earlier. The colours had faded to brown in the sunlight and so I pulled it off.

Turning it over in my hand, I saw that she had written on the back.

To Rosie,
I love you.
From Phoebe

Although she had reached out to me for affection during her time with us, Phoebe had never been verbally demonstrative. To be offered the proof that she had felt such fondness was deeply touching and my eyes brimmed with tears.

Epilogue

What a strange, bittersweet time it is when a child has moved on. In some ways it was a relief to go back to being just the three of us: Jamie, Emily and me. It was lovely to spend some undivided time with both of them but it wasn't an easy transition to make and all of us mourned Phoebe. She had moulded herself a special place in our family and it took us weeks to adjust to the loss.

In my mind the memory of her took on a sepia tone, as Tess and Harry had. It felt as if they all existed on the other side of a locked door, gone and yet always present, like little ghosts. Maxine was true to her word and sent regular texts during the first couple of weeks after Phoebe had moved on, assuring me that she was coping well at her new school and beginning to make friends. It was a huge comfort to learn that she had overcome yet another hurdle in her young life and I felt even more proud of what she'd achieved.

I also had an update from Lenke, something I hadn't expected. She said that the details were sketchy but it seemed the police had bided their time before swooping on the Steadmans' large house in a dawn raid. Nothing damning was found after an initial search and their laptops and PCs also appeared to be clear, but after intensive analysis by the High Tech Crime Unit, officers found hundreds of images of child abuse on the hard drive. The Steadmans had clearly tried, unsuccessfully, to delete the evidence of their crimes.

Although it seemed that they wouldn't be convicted of abusing their daughter, it was a comfort to know that some sort of justice would be served. Robin Steadman had lost his job and now he and his wife would be registered as sex offenders. I hoped the humiliation would haunt them both for the rest of their days.

A date had also been set for the final hearing for sometime in May 2010. Outrageously, I thought, having been charged with the possession of vile images, her parents were continuing to contest the care plan of long-term foster care. They were insistent that Phoebe should be rehabilitated into their care but there was little doubt they would fail, no matter how much money they spent on fancy lawyers, and Lenke was confident of securing a Full Care Order.

Phoebe's new foster carer had pencilled in a reunion date for mid-April, but in late March she wrote saying that Phoebe was still asking to come back to me, so she felt it was too soon for her to cope with a temporary meeting. I convinced myself that Maxine was simply buying time, delaying the news that she intended to cut all ties with us. Though I could understand that as a long-term fosterer she still had all the statutory visits from social workers to put up with and could probably do without yet more people to fit into her schedule, it made me sad to think we wouldn't see her again, not only for us but also for what the sudden ending might do to Phoebe.

But at the beginning of May, characteristic of our whole experience with Phoebe, I got yet another surprise – Maxine rang to say that she now felt confident enough in Phoebe's attachment to her to allow us slowly back into her life. It was a cold day in mid-May when I made the journey to Birmingham to visit them. Emily and Jamie had wanted to come but I felt their presence might be a bit too much for Phoebe to cope with and Maxine had said she preferred to test the water first, and gauge how Phoebe would react when she saw me again.

If the visit went well we had discussed the possibility of establishing a regular meeting, perhaps bi-monthly, so that the children could all stay in touch. Strangely, I felt increasingly nervous as I neared their house. Despite much of the time she had spent with us being fraught with tense emotion, or perhaps even because of it, we had developed a deep bond. It was difficult to tell what effect distance and the passing of time would have on our relationship. Although I had wanted Phoebe to transfer her attachment from me to Maxine, I secretly hoped there was a part of her that still valued the time we had spent together.

As it turned out, I needn't have worried – Phoebe ran out to the car as I pulled into their sweeping driveway, a wide smile on her face. She seemed genuinely pleased to see me, as did Maxine, who was equally welcoming.

'Auntie Rosie!' she said, eager to get the car door open. As I climbed out, she wrapped me in a tight hug then pulled me eagerly into the house to show me the new wallpaper in her bedroom. I spent a lively two hours with the new family, Phoebe filling me in on all the places they'd visited and updating me on the friends she had made in her new school. All the while Maxine kept us supplied with plenty of tea and home-make cake.

When it was time to leave I was pleased that Phoebe wrapped me in a brief hug then reclaimed her rightful place beside Maxine. There were no tears, just a pleading to bring Emily and Jamie along next time, which, with a confirming glance from Maxine, I promised to do.

I knew I would never forget the raw horror of Phoebe's disclosures, but seeing her so happily settled in a new, small but loving family was balm enough to soothe the memory. Maxine walked to the end of the driveway to see me off, clasping one of Phoebe's hands. As I drove away, with the image of them huddled together and waving in my rear-view mirror, I knew I was ready to take on a new challenge.

I resolved that when I got home I would call Des and ask him to put me back on the vacancy register.

* * *

About a year after the move, Phoebe called one day after school to tell me that Maxine had asked if she would like to join the family officially. Social services had agreed that adoption would be in Phoebe's best interests and Phoebe herself was tripping over her words, she was so excited. We were both crying as we spoke on the telephone and laughing at the same time.

And so on a bright summer's day in late summer, Maxine and Phoebe attended court for the adoption hearing. Emily, Jamie and I, having been invited by Maxine to join them for a celebratory lunch, waited outside. The judge presented Phoebe with a new birth certificate and when she emerged from the court she ran down the steps towards us waving the official papers high above her head, a beaming smile on her face.

I was stunned by the change in Phoebe that day. She had gained quite a bit of weight by then and her eyes had completely lost their sunken quality but the transformation was more than physical. I don't know if it was the passing of time that was so healing or the confidence that came with knowing she truly belonged somewhere, but she seemed to walk a few inches taller as she led the way to the restaurant, flanked by Emily and Jamie. I couldn't have been more delighted.

Phoebe is now in a mainstream secondary school, doing well academically, and has developed a passion for art. We still visit the family regularly.